Courtney

By Ted Naifeh

Crumrin

The Night Things

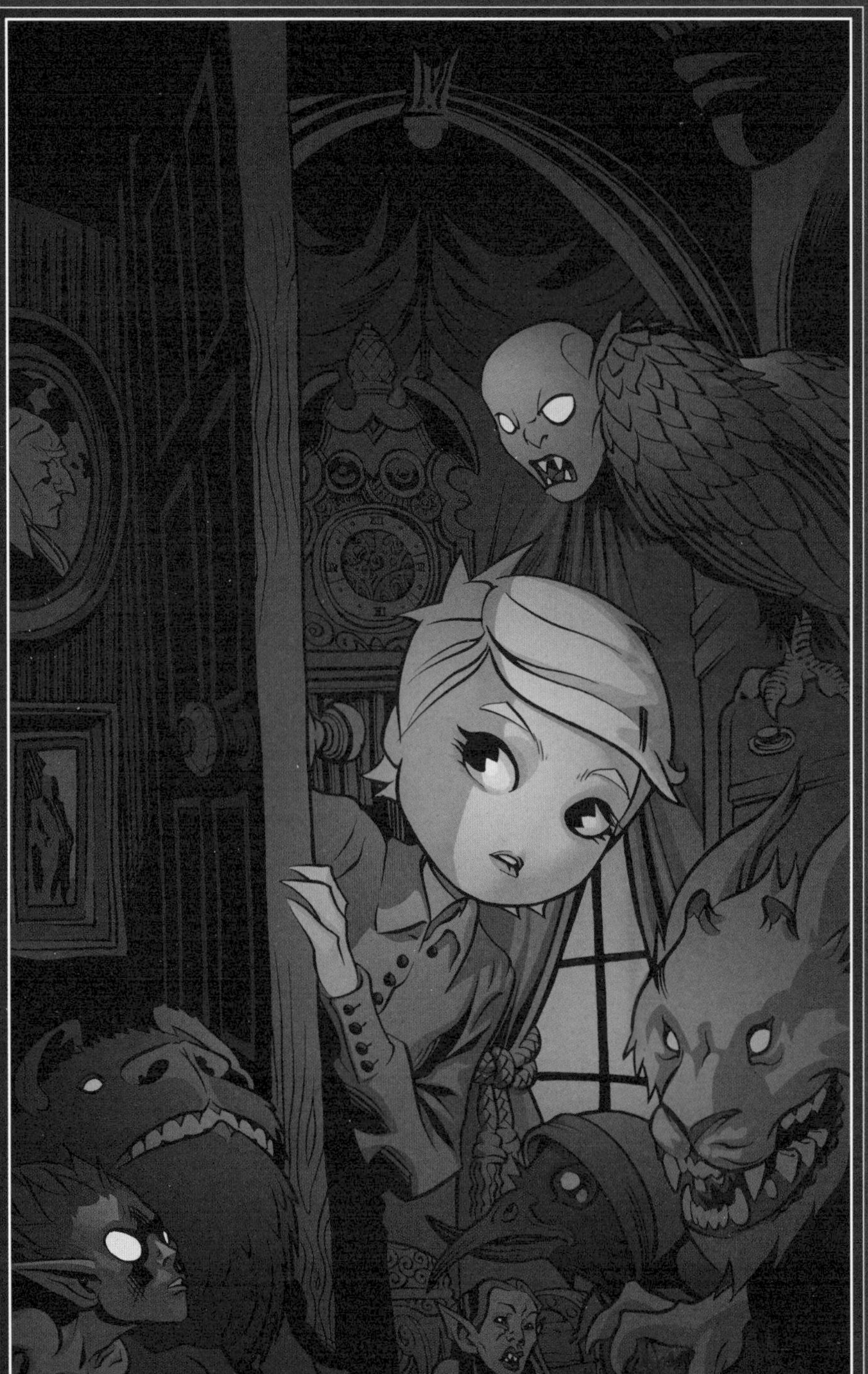

Courtney Crumrin

By Ted Naifeh

The Night Things

Written & Illustrated by

—◈— TED NAIFEH —◈—

Colored by

WARREN WUCINICH

Original Series edited by
JAMES LUCAS JONES

Collection edited by
JILL BEATON

Design by
KEITH WOOD AND ANGIE DOBSON

Oni Press, Inc.

publisher, JOE NOZEMACK

editor in chief, JAMES LUCAS JONES

v.p. of marketing & sales, ANDREW MCINTIRE

sales manager, DAVID DISSANAYAKE

publicity coordinator, RACHEL REED

director of design & production, TROY LOOK

graphic designer, HILARY THOMPSON

digital prepress technician, ANGIE DOBSON

managing editor, ARI YARWOOD

senior editor, CHARLIE CHU

editor, ROBIN HERRERA

administrative assistant, ALISSA SALLAH

director of logistics, BRAD ROOKS

logistics associate, JUNG LEE

Originally published as issues 1-4 of the Oni Press comic series
Courtney Crumrin and the Night Things.

1305 SE Martin Luther King Jr. Blvd.
Suite A
Portland, OR 97214

www.onipress.com

First Edition: June 2017

ISBN 978-1-62010-419-4
eISBN 978-1-62010-182-7

1 3 5 7 9 10 8 6 4 2

Library of Congress Control Number: 2011933140

Printed in Singapore.

To Magic, for helping awaken my imagination, and to Ron,
for telling me of the Night Things.

A Few Words About Children, Nightmares, And Outcasts

Childhood is a much darker world than most adults care to remember. If anything, childhood is even more full of terror and passion than life becomes after a few decades spent killing off brain cells. Small children are straight outta nature, all id, tribal survivalists to the core. They drive the weak away from the village, instinctively hating those who are different, ugly, or slow. Sure, they're preoccupied with stockpiling toys instead of guns, but the principle is always the same. Behind the big shiny eyes and dimples is The Lord of the Flies, ticking and buzzing. We learn sweetness and the ability to sit still later on in order to fit into society and get grown-up things like jobs and apartments and girl- or boyfriends, things that seem yucky and boring until the moment we're ready for them. Among the byproducts that boil off and are lost in the process of growing up are simplicity, lots of dreams, and a huge amount of fear.

Children understand fear. But there are also childhood terrors that go even deeper than the social torture experienced daily in every grammar school in the world. One of the worst nightmares I ever had seemed to be trying to explain the bedtime fears that all kids go through. While I was asleep, my brain told me a story about children and their common, silly childhood fears: the dark, the bogeyman, the creature in the closet, the monster under the bed. The stuff we learn to laugh at and later humor and comfort in our own children. Then I saw the human predators, the real-life monsters such as serial killers and child murderers, and their helpless prey. My mind suggested that it was the terror suffered by these victims that, via some kind of collective unconscious, shows up as the Thing at the Foot of the Bed. That even the most sheltered kid lovingly tucked in every night somehow knows about these very real bogeymen and feels the horror of the unlucky ones, the ones who got caught. At 4 a.m. I woke up screaming and sat with all the lights on and my back to the wall until the watery winter sun came up. I'd never been so glad to be an adult before.

Strangely enough, despite all of the more or less real terrors they contend with on a daily and nightly basis, children love to be scared, love to be grossed out, love, above all, to be shocked.

The only children's stories that are truly classic, timeless, and beloved are also subversively honest about life's ugliness. Kids experience reality on a much simpler level than adults, and don't buy stories that are too sugary. They're realists in the sense that they know there's much more to reality than what we see around us every day or what we learn in school. There almost has to be a tragic, a bitter, or a vicious edge to the story, or they know it for the load of bull it is. Mark Twain, Roald Dahl, and Judy Blume, three of the all-time best-beloved children's authors, knew this. Their books are often banned from schools and libraries because of parents' need to believe that children are innocent of pain and cruelty and can be protected from knowledge about the darkness of human nature.

I grew up on those and other great authors, whose books gave me a glimpse at life's beautiful and horrible truths. Now that I'm an adult, at least in the sense that I have to pay taxes and worry about gingivitis, I see that I'm a part of the diaspora of kids that was driven from the village, for various reasons, and spent adolescence observing it all from the outside. We've formed our own tribes, and as far as I can see, we, the geeks, won. We're smarter, we're independent, we're more courageous, and we value each other more than the kids who fit in without effort, blending in and never really getting to know themselves. I only wish I could tell my little sister, who's about Courtney's age, and rapidly moving from the unicorn stage to the moody poetry stage and reading everything she can get her hands on, to hang in there. Sure, it'll be a rough eight or ten years, but at the end of it, she'll be a conscious, brilliant, confident woman with a loving, like-minded community and her own unique style. It's worth the pain you feel now. Trust me. And grown-up geekboys do make the best partners. I should know.

Actually, come to think of it, that doesn't sound particularly comforting— eight years is a lifetime to a kid. And of course, you can't tell kids anything.

—KELLY CRUMRIN, FALL 2002

Kelly Crumrin is a freelance writer who lives in San Francisco and would head the campaign to elect Emperor Norton as president if only he weren't so dead.

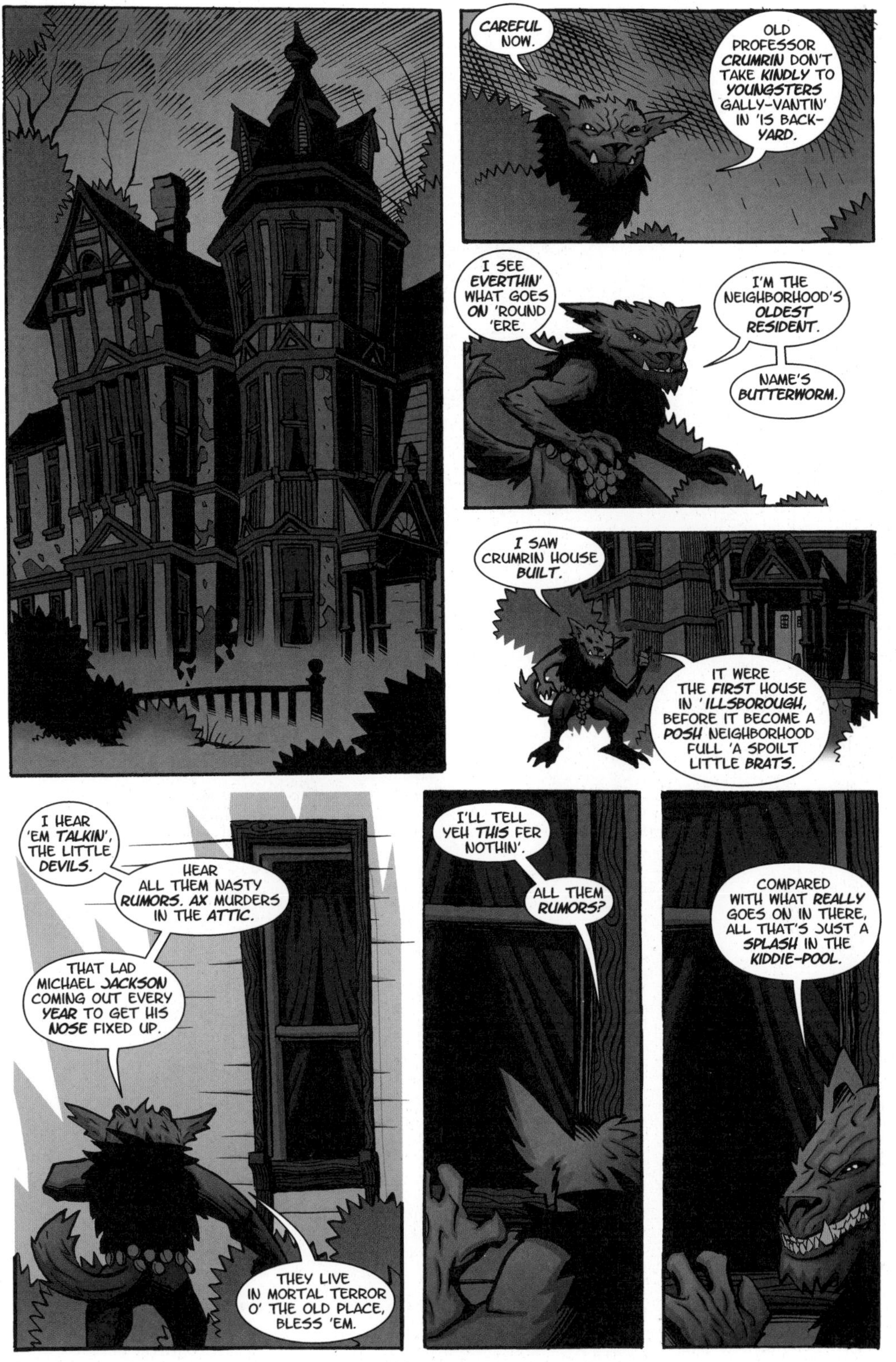
CAREFUL NOW.
OLD PROFESSOR CRUMRIN DON'T TAKE KINDLY TO YOUNGSTERS GALLY-VANTIN' IN 'IS BACK-YARD.
I SEE EVERTHIN' WHAT GOES ON 'ROUND 'ERE.
I'M THE NEIGHBORHOOD'S OLDEST RESIDENT.
NAME'S BUTTERWORM.
I SAW CRUMRIN HOUSE BUILT.
IT WERE THE FIRST HOUSE IN 'ILLSBOROUGH, BEFORE IT BECOME A POSH NEIGHBORHOOD FULL 'A SPOILT LITTLE BRATS.
I HEAR 'EM TALKIN', THE LITTLE DEVILS.
HEAR ALL THEM NASTY RUMORS. AX MURDERS IN THE ATTIC.
THAT LAD MICHAEL JACKSON COMING OUT EVERY YEAR TO GET HIS NOSE FIXED UP.
THEY LIVE IN MORTAL TERROR O' THE OLD PLACE, BLESS 'EM.
I'LL TELL YEH THIS FER NOTHIN'.
ALL THEM RUMORS?
COMPARED WITH WHAT REALLY GOES ON IN THERE, ALL THAT'S JUST A SPLASH IN THE KIDDIE-POOL.

Chapter One

DO YOU KNOW THAT *LITTLE BOROUGH* OUTSIDE THE CITY, THE ONE WITH ALL THE BIG MANSIONS AND TREES?

DO YOU KNOW THAT *ONE HOUSE*, THE MOST TALKED ABOUT HOUSE IN THE *WHOLE NEIGHBORHOOD?*

NOT THE FANCY MARBLE-COLUMNED *OUDLER MANSION*, NOR *RADLEY HALL* WHERE PRESIDENT NIXON ONCE DINED IN THE SEVENTIES. NO, I'M REFERRING TO THE HOUSE OF OLD *ALOYSIUS CRUMRIN*.

IT IS WELL KNOWN THAT *TERRIBLE* THINGS HAPPEN THERE, AND THAT OLD MAN CRUMRIN IS MADDER THAN A *VICTORIAN HATMAKER.*

WELL, THAT'S THE HOUSE THAT *COURTNEY CRUMRIN* WOULD SOON BE CALLING HOME.

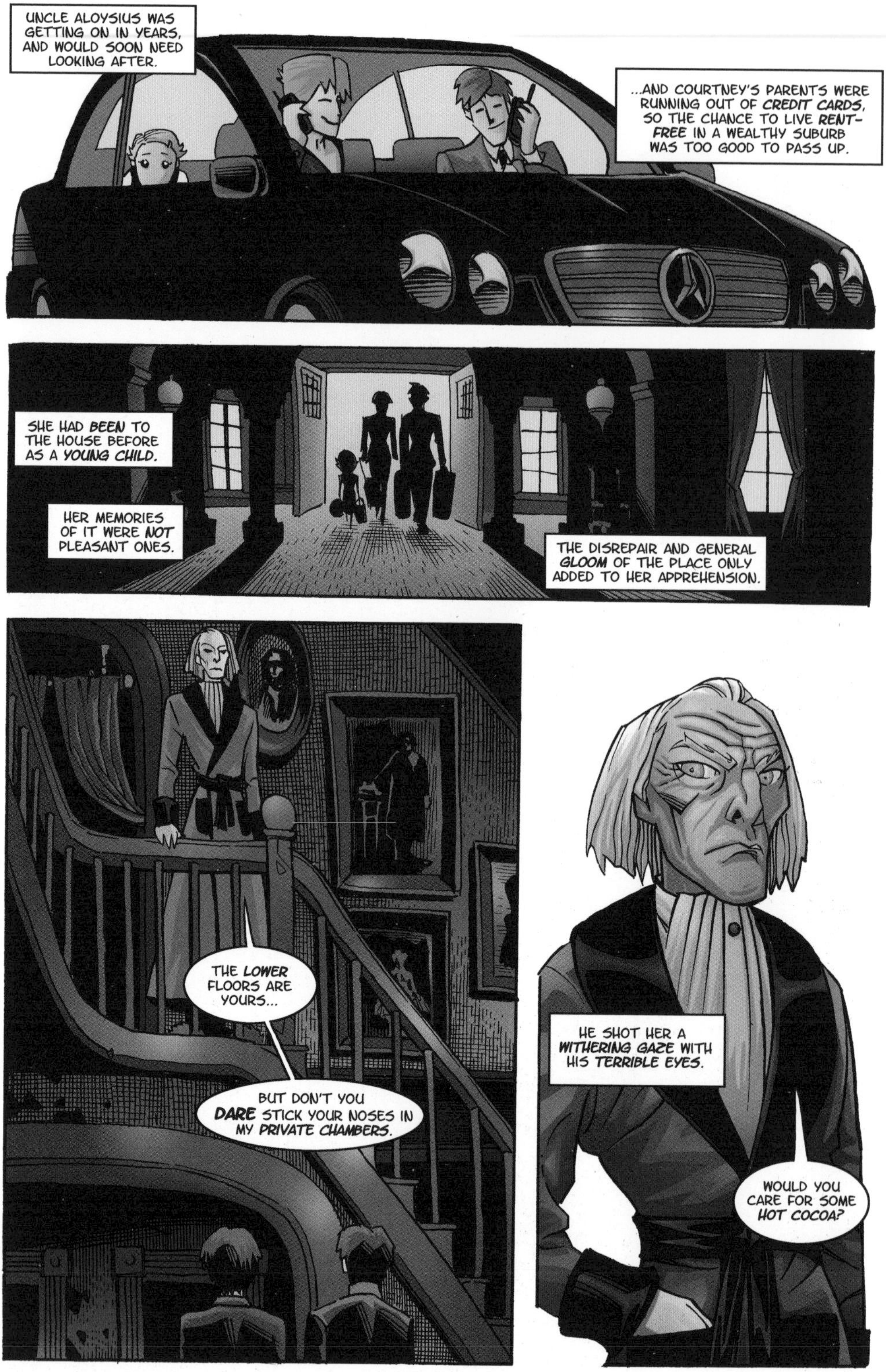
UNCLE ALOYSIUS WAS GETTING ON IN YEARS, AND WOULD SOON NEED LOOKING AFTER.
...AND COURTNEY'S PARENTS WERE RUNNING OUT OF *CREDIT CARDS*, SO THE CHANCE TO LIVE *RENT-FREE* IN A WEALTHY SUBURB WAS TOO GOOD TO PASS UP.
SHE HAD *BEEN* TO THE HOUSE BEFORE AS A *YOUNG CHILD.*
HER MEMORIES OF IT WERE *NOT* PLEASANT ONES.
THE DISREPAIR AND GENERAL *GLOOM* OF THE PLACE ONLY ADDED TO HER APPREHENSION.
THE *LOWER* FLOORS ARE YOURS...
BUT DON'T YOU **DARE** STICK YOUR NOSES IN MY *PRIVATE CHAMBERS.*
HE SHOT HER A *WITHERING GAZE* WITH HIS *TERRIBLE EYES.*
WOULD YOU CARE FOR SOME *HOT COCOA?*

NO, THANK YOU, SIR.

UNCLE ALOYSIUS WAS EVEN *NASTIER* THAN SHE REMEMBERED HIM, WITH A FACE THAT WOULD CURDLE *NEW MILK*.

THE PROSPECT OF LIVING UNDER HIS ROOF BEGAN TO *SINK IN* THEN, AND COURTNEY'S *STOMACH* TURNED TO *ICEWATER*.

"I MUST HAVE BEEN REALLY *ROTTEN* IN MY PREVIOUS LIFE," THOUGHT COURTNEY.

"MAYBE A *GYM TEACHER*."

HER ROOM WAS COLD, DUSTY AND COMFORTLESS. COURTNEY DEALT WITH HER DISAPPOINTMENT THE BEST WAY SHE KNEW HOW...

...GRUMBLE...

IT WAS DIFFICULT TO SLEEP, FOR THE COVERS SMELLED OF *AGE*, AND THE HOUSE'S TIMBERS EMITTED *STRANGE CREAKS* AND *GROANS*.

BUT MORE ALARMING *BY FAR* WAS THE SOUND OF SOMETHING *STIRRING* AT THE FOOT OF HER BED.

WHO'S THERE!?!

AT FIRST SHE COULDN'T REMEMBER WHERE SHE WAS.

BUT AS WAKEFULNESS TOOK HOLD, A SINGLE STRAY DREAM SEEMED TO REMAIN.

CONFUSED THOUGHTS STRUGGLED IN HER SLEEPY MIND TO EXPLAIN WHAT SHE WAS SEEING.

IT WASN'T TILL SHE HAD THE LIGHT ON THAT ICY PANIC BEGAN TO TAKE HOLD.

HUH ...

NEEDLESS TO SAY, SHE DIDN'T CLOSE HER EYES AGAIN *ALL NIGHT.* WOULD YOU?

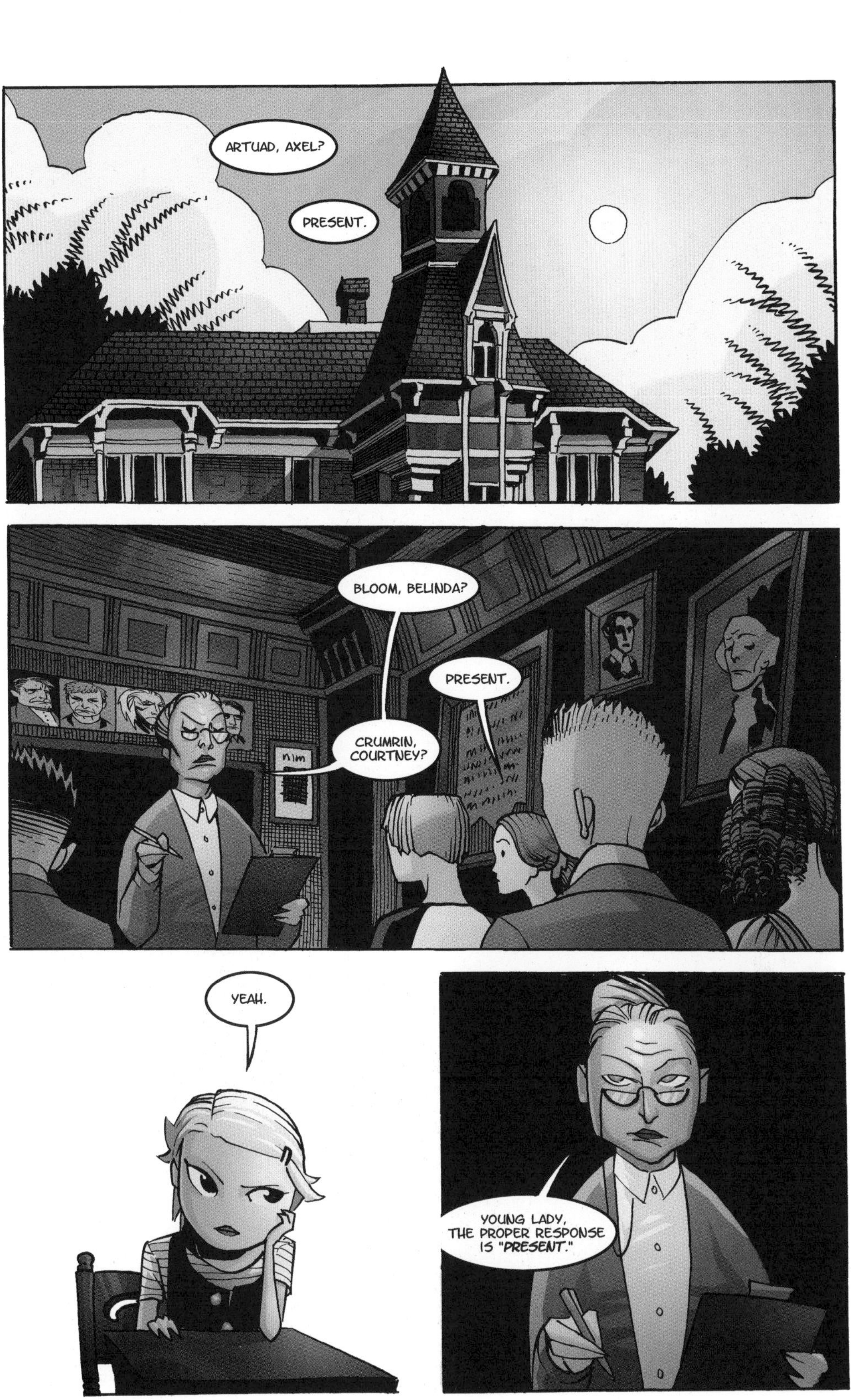
ARTUAD, AXEL?
PRESENT.
BLOOM, BELINDA?
PRESENT.
CRUMRIN, COURTNEY?
YEAH.
YOUNG LADY, THE PROPER RESPONSE IS "*PRESENT*."

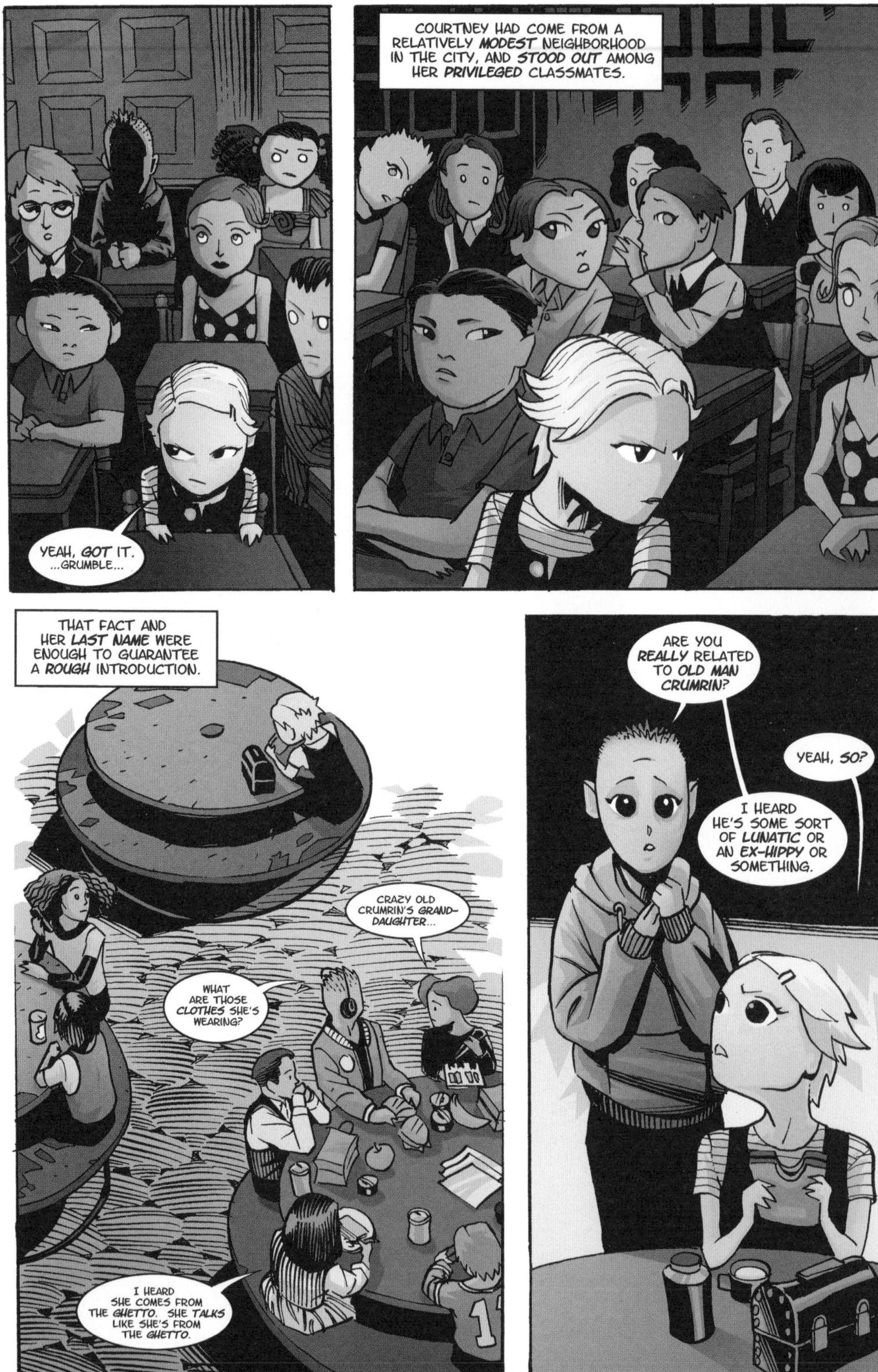
YEAH, GOT IT.
...GRUMBLE...
COURTNEY HAD COME FROM A RELATIVELY MODEST NEIGHBORHOOD IN THE CITY, AND STOOD OUT AMONG HER PRIVILEGED CLASSMATES.
THAT FACT AND HER LAST NAME WERE ENOUGH TO GUARANTEE A ROUGH INTRODUCTION.
CRAZY OLD CRUMRIN'S GRAND-DAUGHTER...
WHAT ARE THOSE CLOTHES SHE'S WEARING?
I HEARD SHE COMES FROM THE GHETTO. SHE TALKS LIKE SHE'S FROM THE GHETTO.
ARE YOU REALLY RELATED TO OLD MAN CRUMRIN?
YEAH, SO?
I HEARD HE'S SOME SORT OF LUNATIC OR AN EX-HIPPY OR SOMETHING.

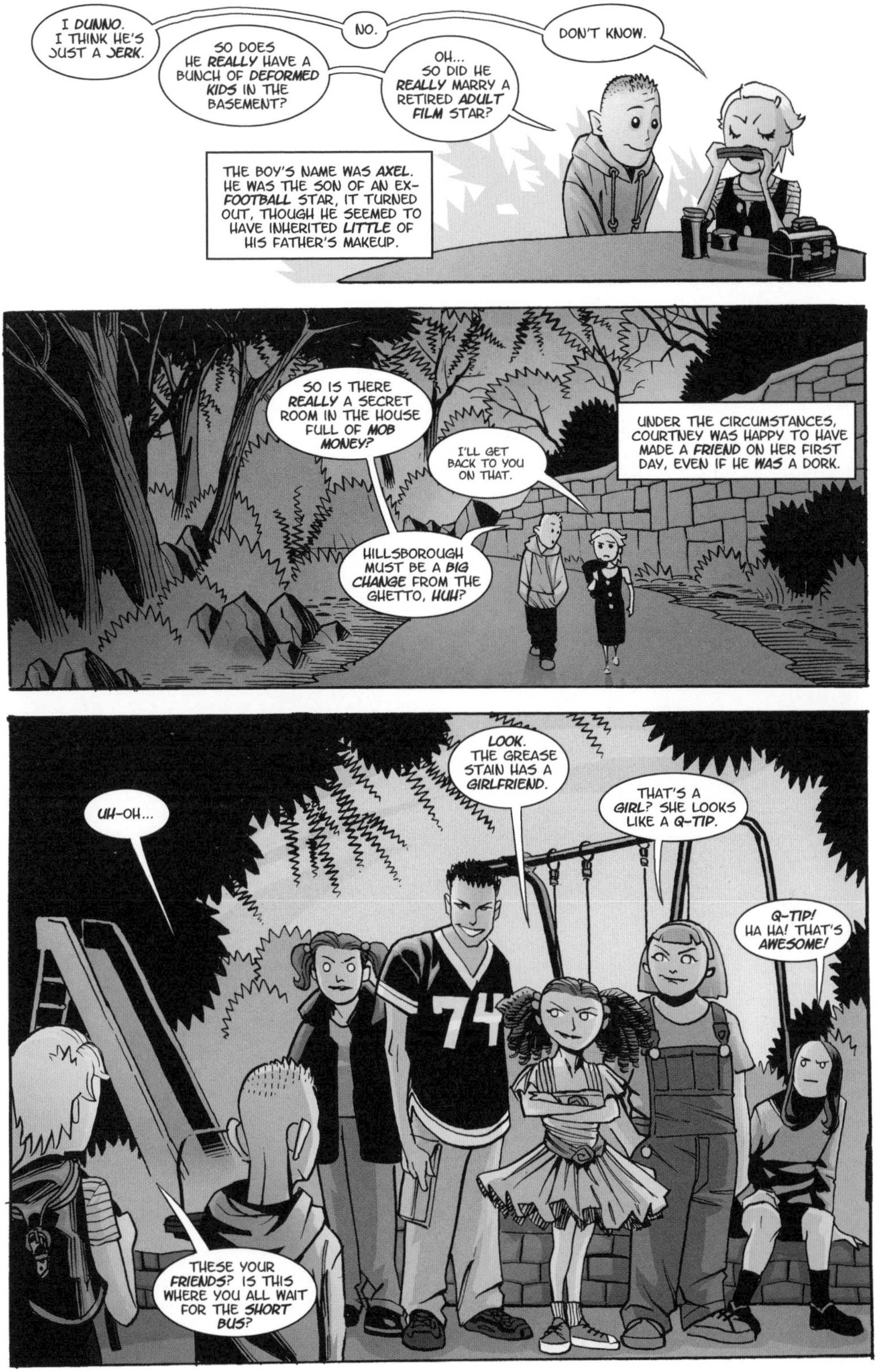
I DUNNO. I THINK HE'S JUST A JERK.
SO DOES HE REALLY HAVE A BUNCH OF DEFORMED KIDS IN THE BASEMENT?
NO.
OH... SO DID HE REALLY MARRY A RETIRED ADULT FILM STAR?
DON'T KNOW.
THE BOY'S NAME WAS AXEL. HE WAS THE SON OF AN EX-FOOTBALL STAR, IT TURNED OUT, THOUGH HE SEEMED TO HAVE INHERITED LITTLE OF HIS FATHER'S MAKEUP.
UNDER THE CIRCUMSTANCES, COURTNEY WAS HAPPY TO HAVE MADE A FRIEND ON HER FIRST DAY, EVEN IF HE WAS A DORK.
SO IS THERE REALLY A SECRET ROOM IN THE HOUSE FULL OF MOB MONEY?
I'LL GET BACK TO YOU ON THAT.
HILLSBOROUGH MUST BE A BIG CHANGE FROM THE GHETTO, HUH?
UH-OH...
LOOK. THE GREASE STAIN HAS A GIRLFRIEND.
THAT'S A GIRL? SHE LOOKS LIKE A Q-TIP.
Q-TIP! HA HA! THAT'S AWESOME!
74
THESE YOUR FRIENDS? IS THIS WHERE YOU ALL WAIT FOR THE SHORT BUS?

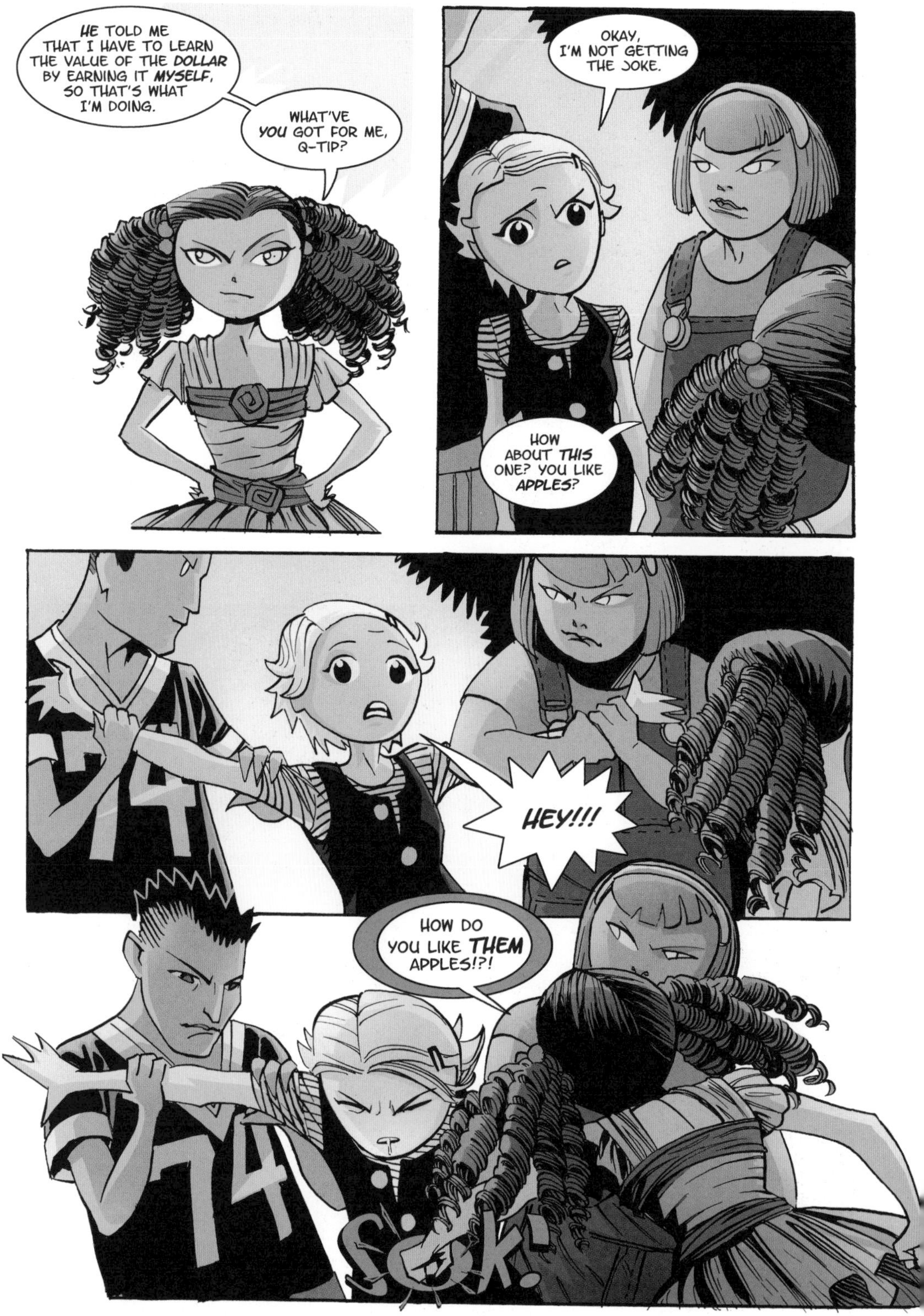
HE TOLD ME THAT I HAVE TO LEARN THE VALUE OF THE DOLLAR BY EARNING IT MYSELF, SO THAT'S WHAT I'M DOING.
WHAT'VE YOU GOT FOR ME, Q-TIP?
OKAY, I'M NOT GETTING THE JOKE.
HOW ABOUT THIS ONE? YOU LIKE APPLES?
HEY!!!
HOW DO YOU LIKE THEM APPLES!?!
SOCK!

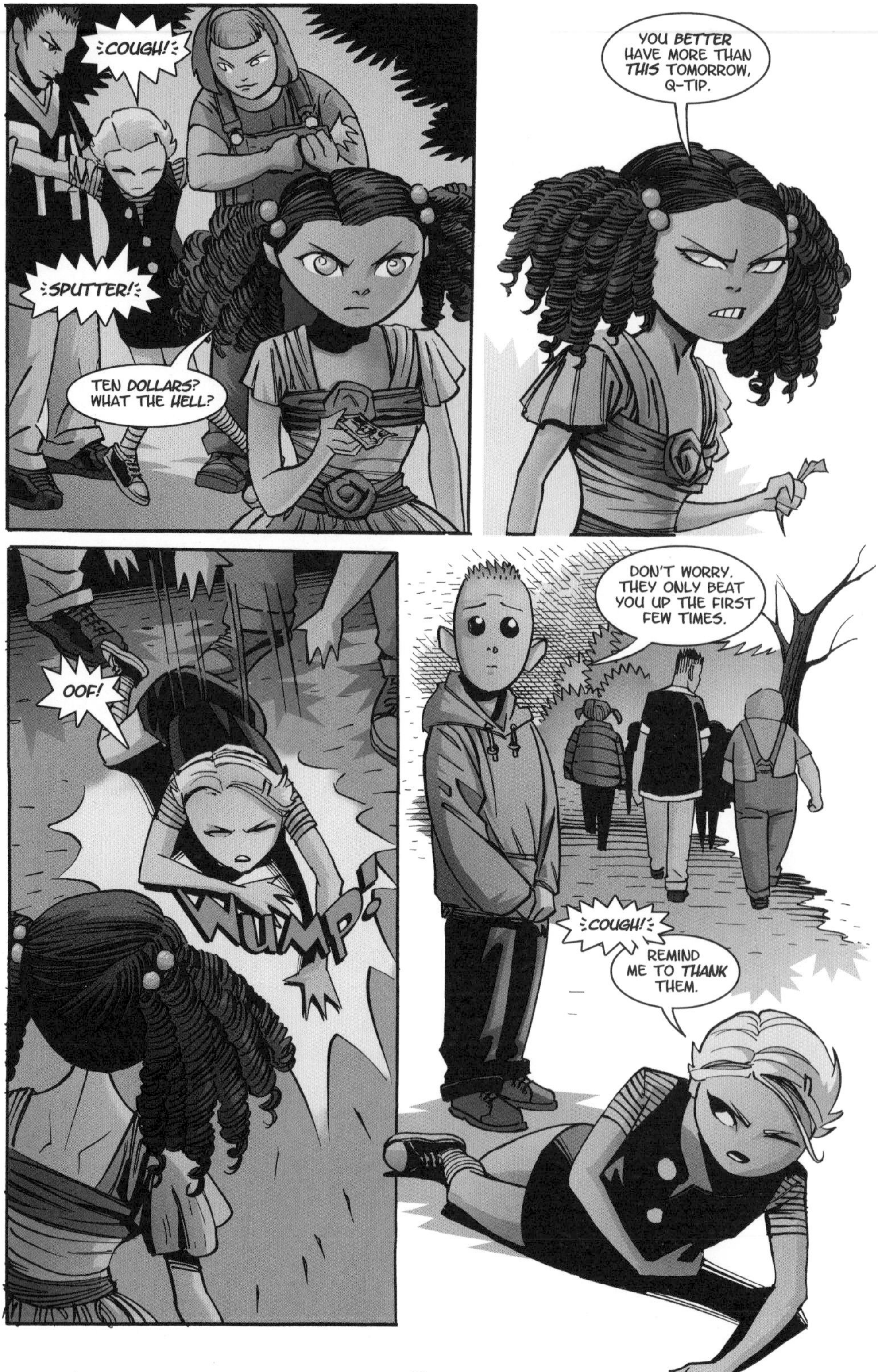
COUGH!
SPUTTER!
TEN DOLLARS? WHAT THE HELL?
YOU BETTER HAVE MORE THAN THIS TOMORROW, Q-TIP.
OOF!
WUMP!
DON'T WORRY. THEY ONLY BEAT YOU UP THE FIRST FEW TIMES.
COUGH!
REMIND ME TO THANK THEM.

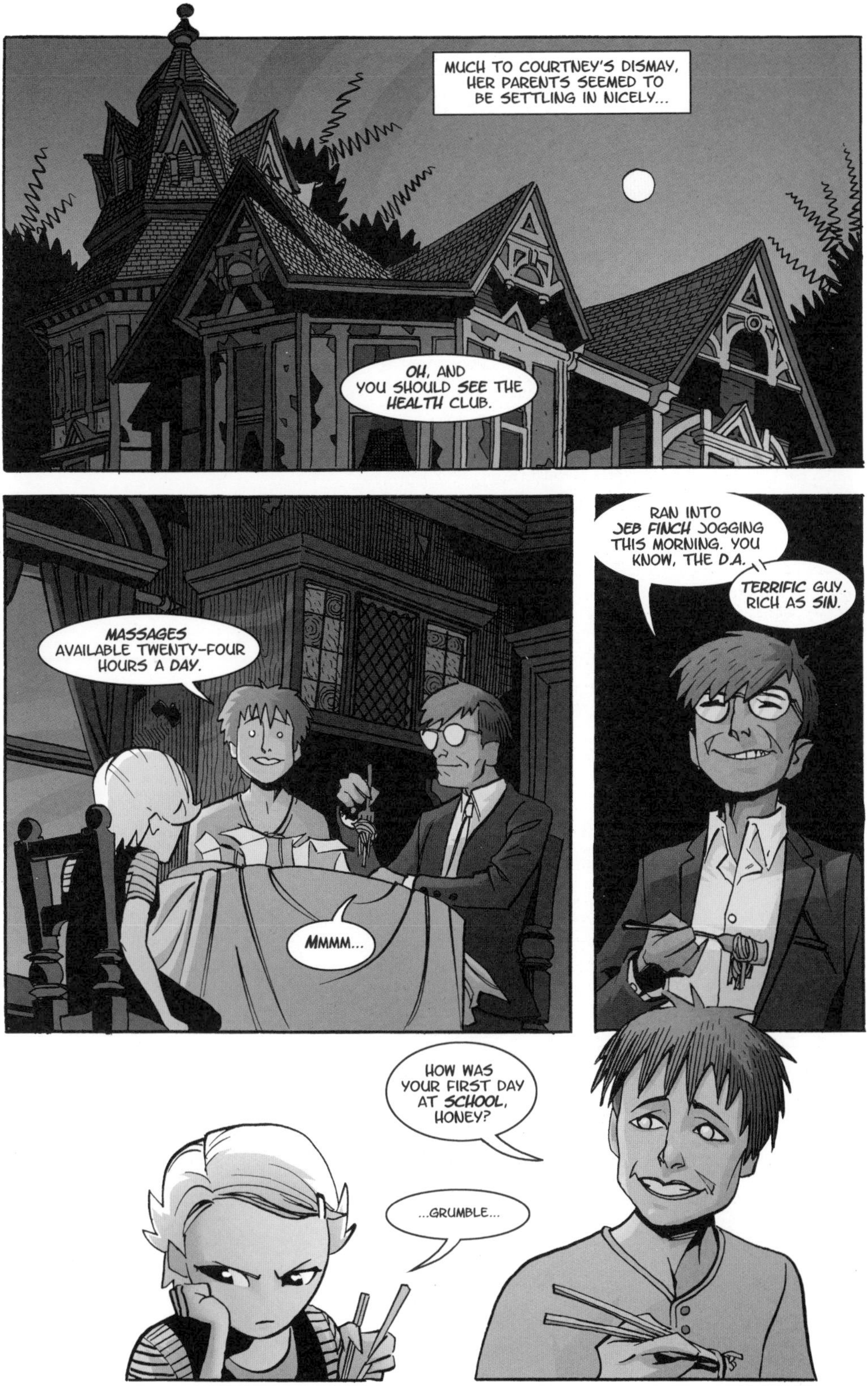
MUCH TO COURTNEY'S DISMAY, HER PARENTS SEEMED TO BE SETTLING IN NICELY...
OH, AND YOU SHOULD SEE THE HEALTH CLUB.
MASSAGES AVAILABLE TWENTY-FOUR HOURS A DAY.
MMMM...
RAN INTO JEB FINCH JOGGING THIS MORNING. YOU KNOW, THE D.A.
TERRIFIC GUY. RICH AS SIN.
HOW WAS YOUR FIRST DAY AT SCHOOL, HONEY?
...GRUMBLE...

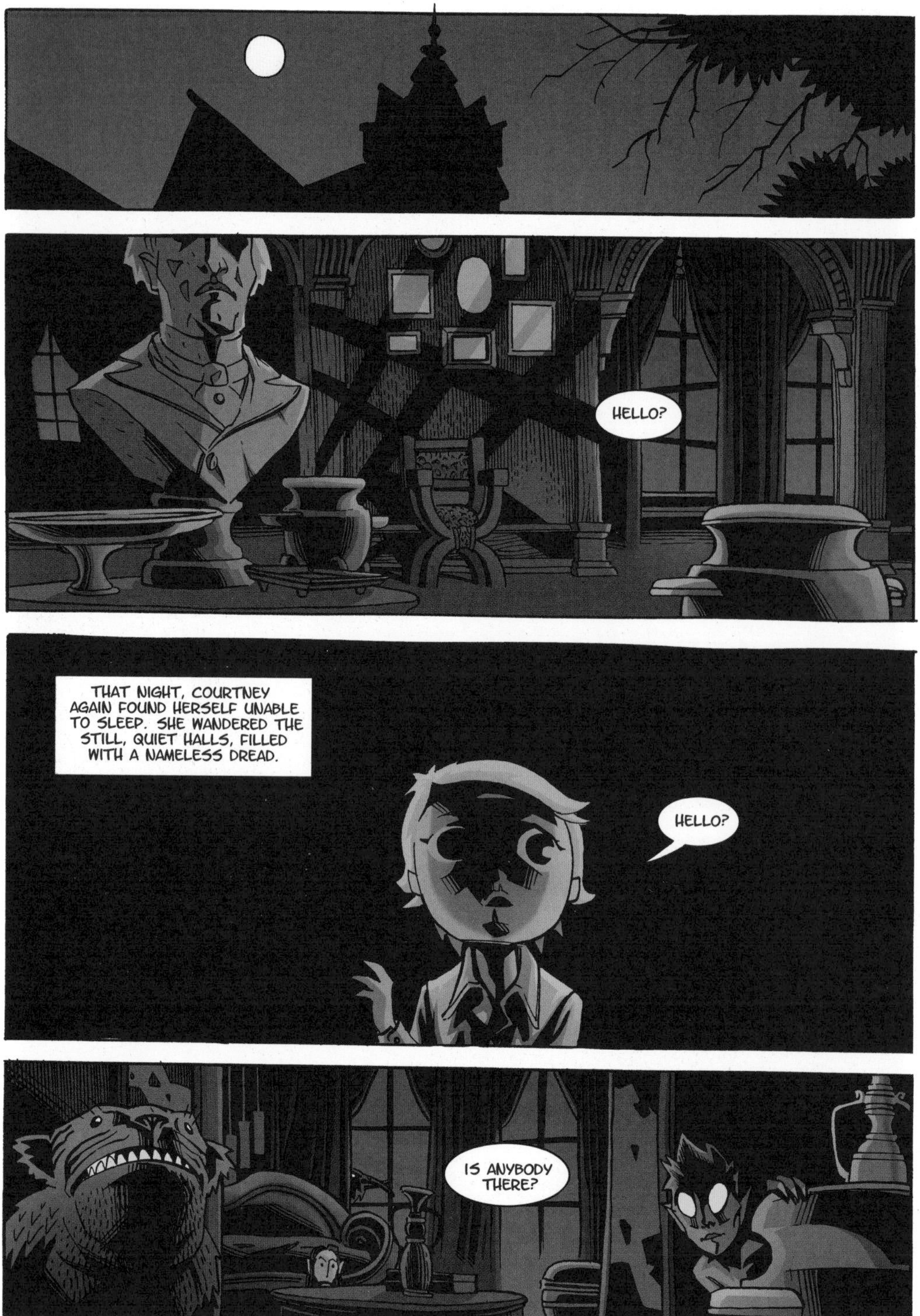
HELLO?
THAT NIGHT, COURTNEY AGAIN FOUND HERSELF UNABLE TO SLEEP. SHE WANDERED THE STILL, QUIET HALLS, FILLED WITH A NAMELESS DREAD.
HELLO?
IS ANYBODY THERE?

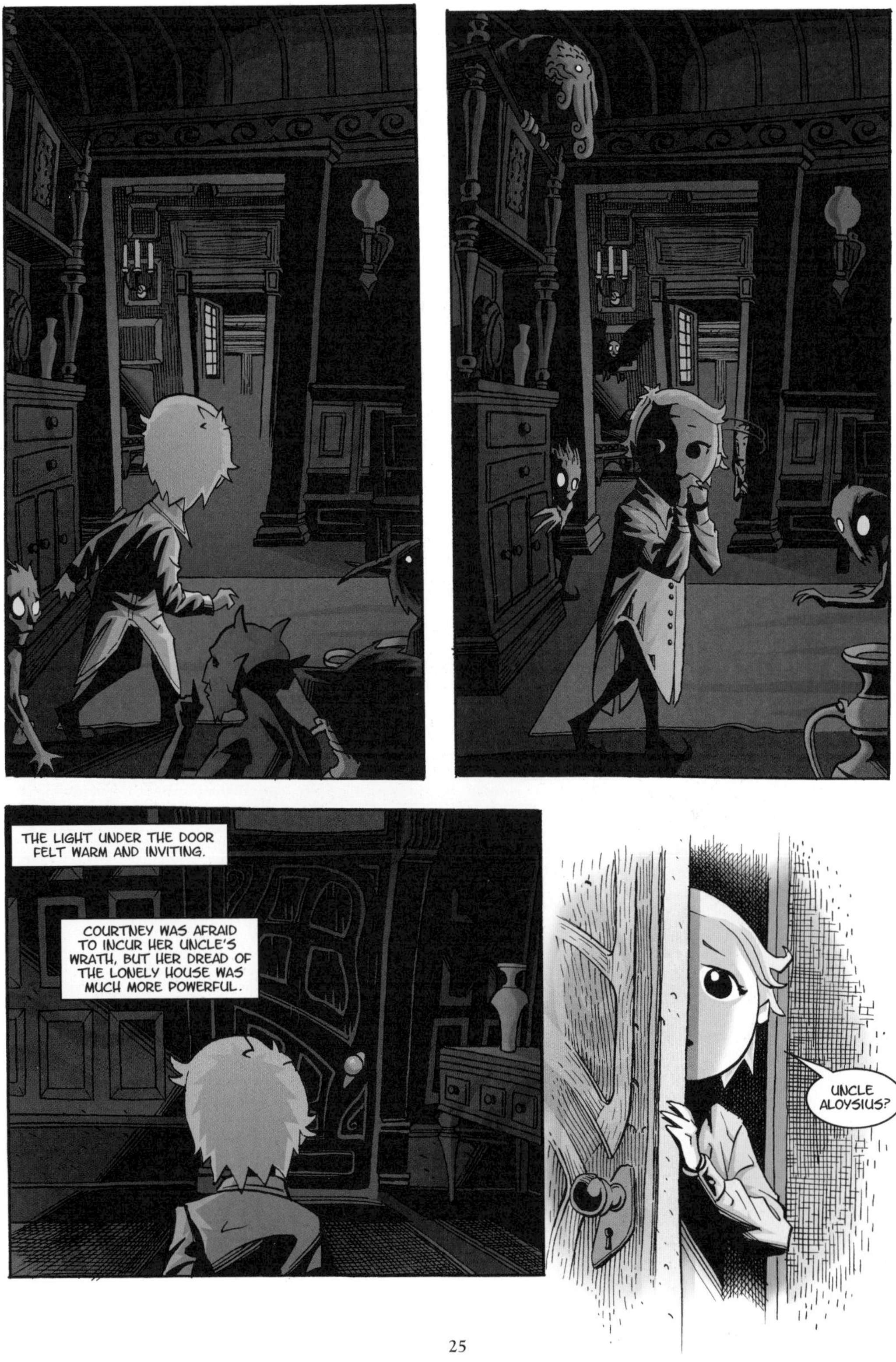
THE LIGHT UNDER THE DOOR FELT WARM AND INVITING.
COURTNEY WAS AFRAID TO INCUR HER UNCLE'S WRATH, BUT HER DREAD OF THE LONELY HOUSE WAS MUCH MORE POWERFUL.
UNCLE ALOYSIUS?

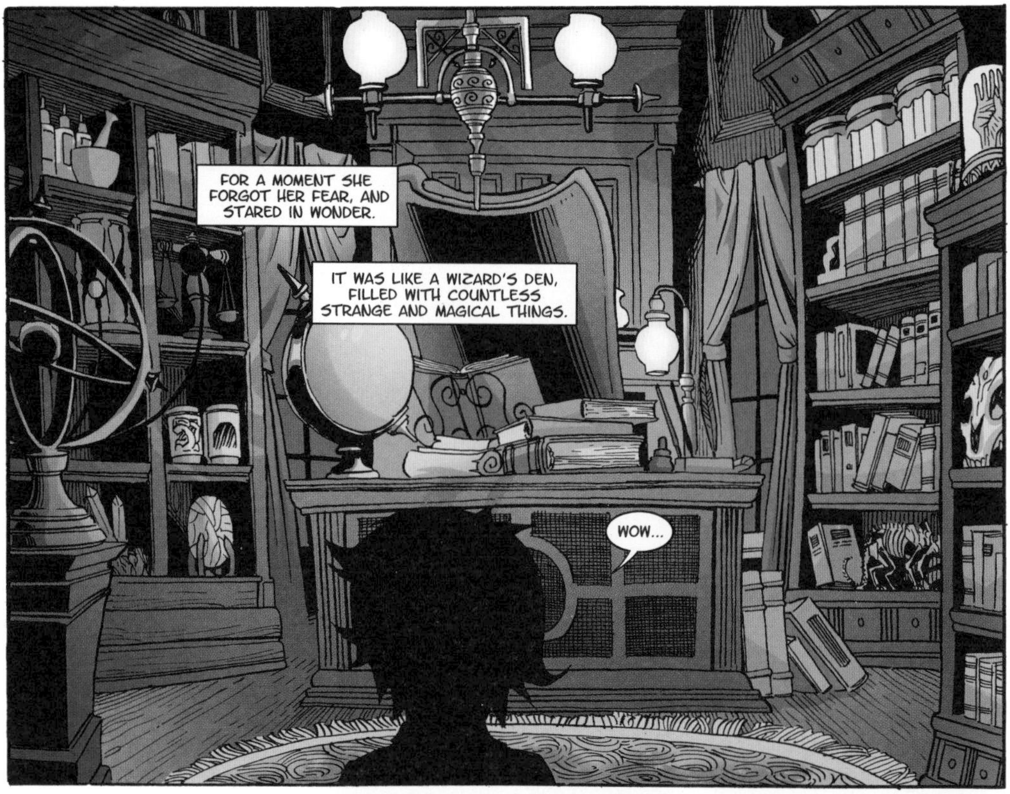
FOR A MOMENT SHE FORGOT HER FEAR, AND STARED IN WONDER.
IT WAS LIKE A WIZARD'S DEN, FILLED WITH COUNTLESS STRANGE AND MAGICAL THINGS.
WOW...

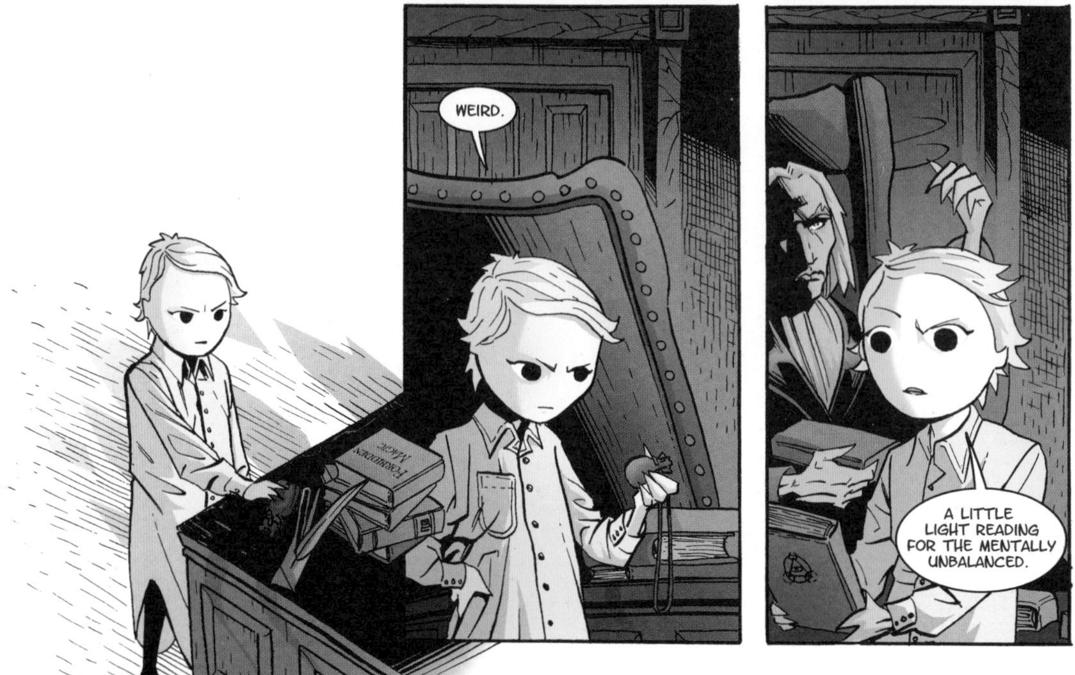
WEIRD.
A LITTLE LIGHT READING FOR THE MENTALLY UNBALANCED.

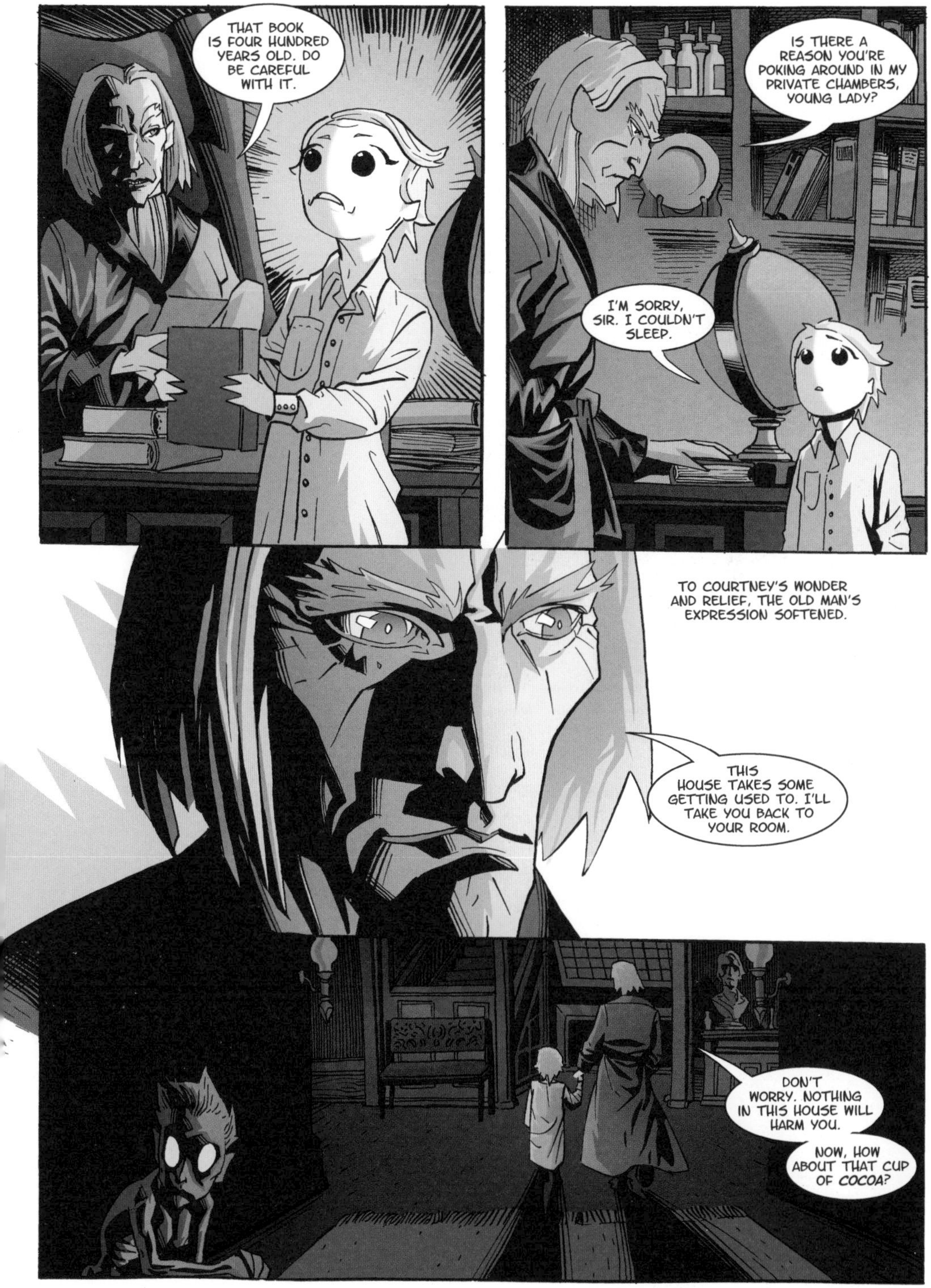
THAT BOOK IS FOUR HUNDRED YEARS OLD. DO BE CAREFUL WITH IT.
IS THERE A REASON YOU'RE POKING AROUND IN MY PRIVATE CHAMBERS, YOUNG LADY?
I'M SORRY, SIR. I COULDN'T SLEEP.
TO COURTNEY'S WONDER AND RELIEF, THE OLD MAN'S EXPRESSION SOFTENED.
THIS HOUSE TAKES SOME GETTING USED TO. I'LL TAKE YOU BACK TO YOUR ROOM.
DON'T WORRY. NOTHING IN THIS HOUSE WILL HARM YOU.
NOW, HOW ABOUT THAT CUP OF *COCOA*?

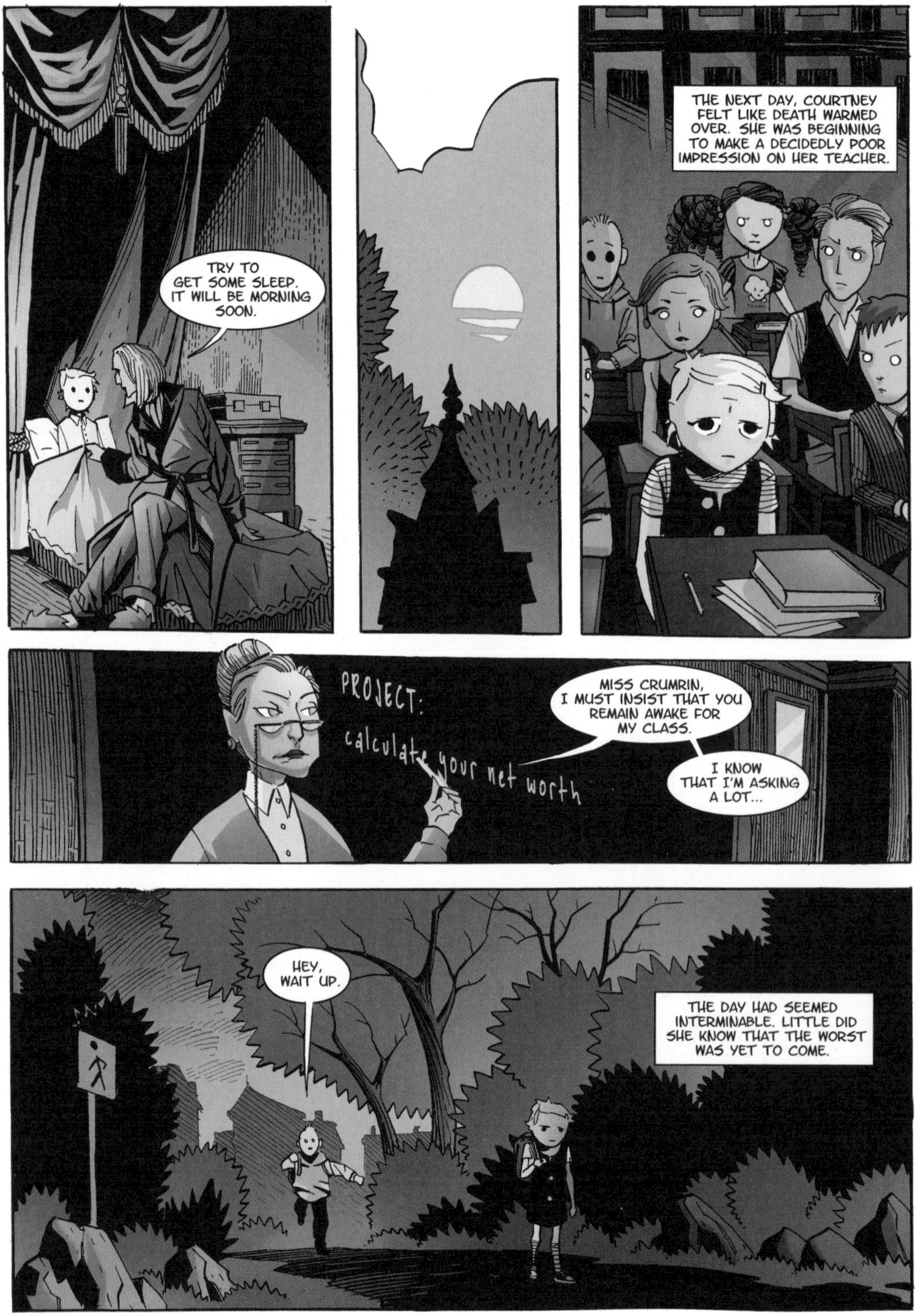
TRY TO GET SOME SLEEP. IT WILL BE MORNING SOON.
THE NEXT DAY, COURTNEY FELT LIKE DEATH WARMED OVER. SHE WAS BEGINNING TO MAKE A DECIDEDLY POOR IMPRESSION ON HER TEACHER.
PROJECT:
calculate your net worth
MISS CRUMRIN, I MUST INSIST THAT YOU REMAIN AWAKE FOR MY CLASS.
I KNOW THAT I'M ASKING A LOT...
HEY, WAIT UP.
THE DAY HAD SEEMED INTERMINABLE. LITTLE DID SHE KNOW THAT THE WORST WAS YET TO COME.

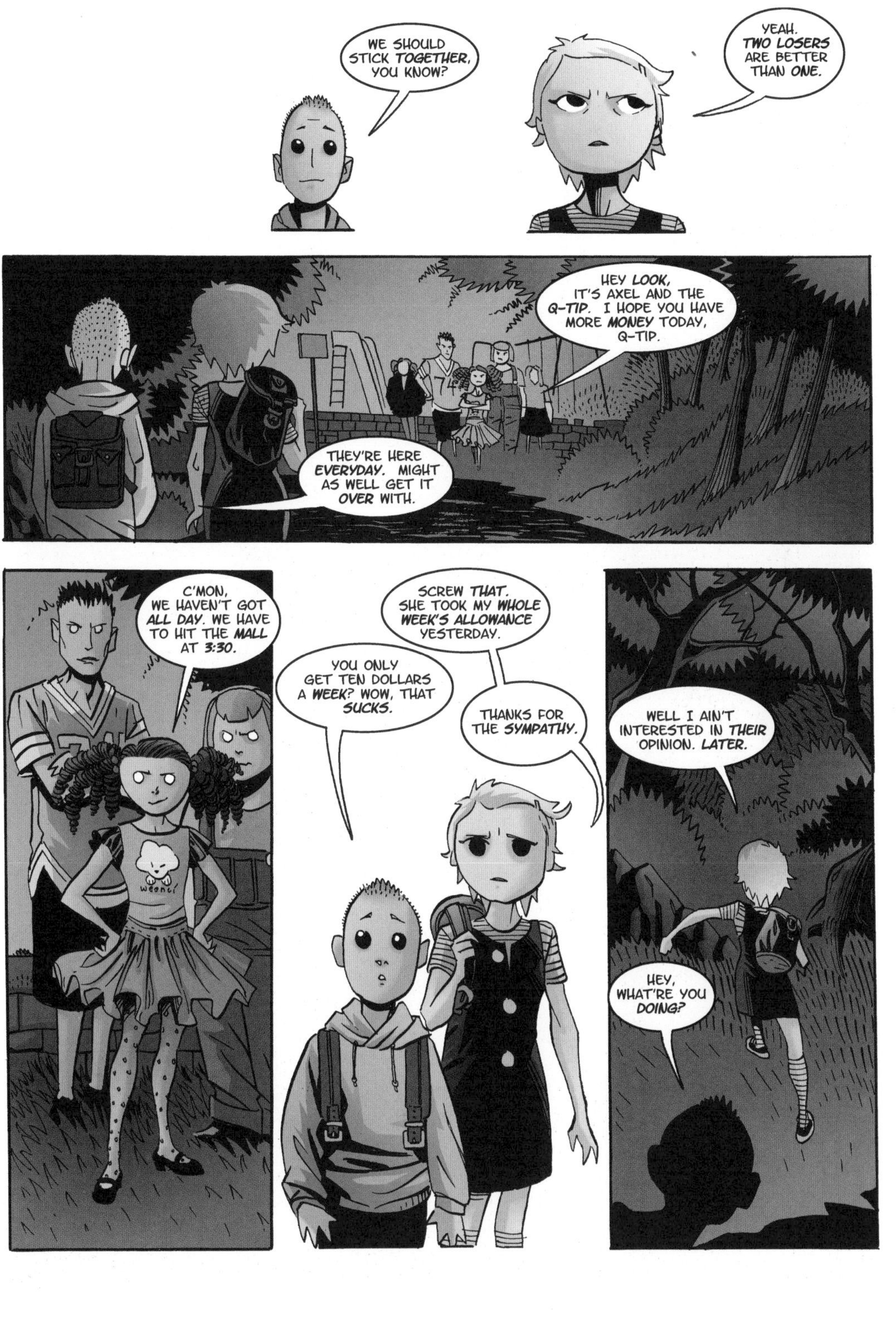
WE SHOULD STICK TOGETHER, YOU KNOW?
YEAH. TWO LOSERS ARE BETTER THAN ONE.
HEY LOOK, IT'S AXEL AND THE Q-TIP. I HOPE YOU HAVE MORE MONEY TODAY, Q-TIP.
THEY'RE HERE EVERYDAY. MIGHT AS WELL GET IT OVER WITH.
C'MON, WE HAVEN'T GOT ALL DAY. WE HAVE TO HIT THE MALL AT 3:30.
SCREW THAT. SHE TOOK MY WHOLE WEEK'S ALLOWANCE YESTERDAY.
YOU ONLY GET TEN DOLLARS A WEEK? WOW, THAT SUCKS.
THANKS FOR THE SYMPATHY.
WELL I AIN'T INTERESTED IN THEIR OPINION. LATER.
HEY, WHAT'RE YOU DOING?

COURTNEY HEARD AXEL'S FOOTSTEPS FADE BEHIND HER AS SHE PLUNGED DEEPER AND DEEPER INTO THE TREES. HIS CALLS SLOWLY RECEDED.

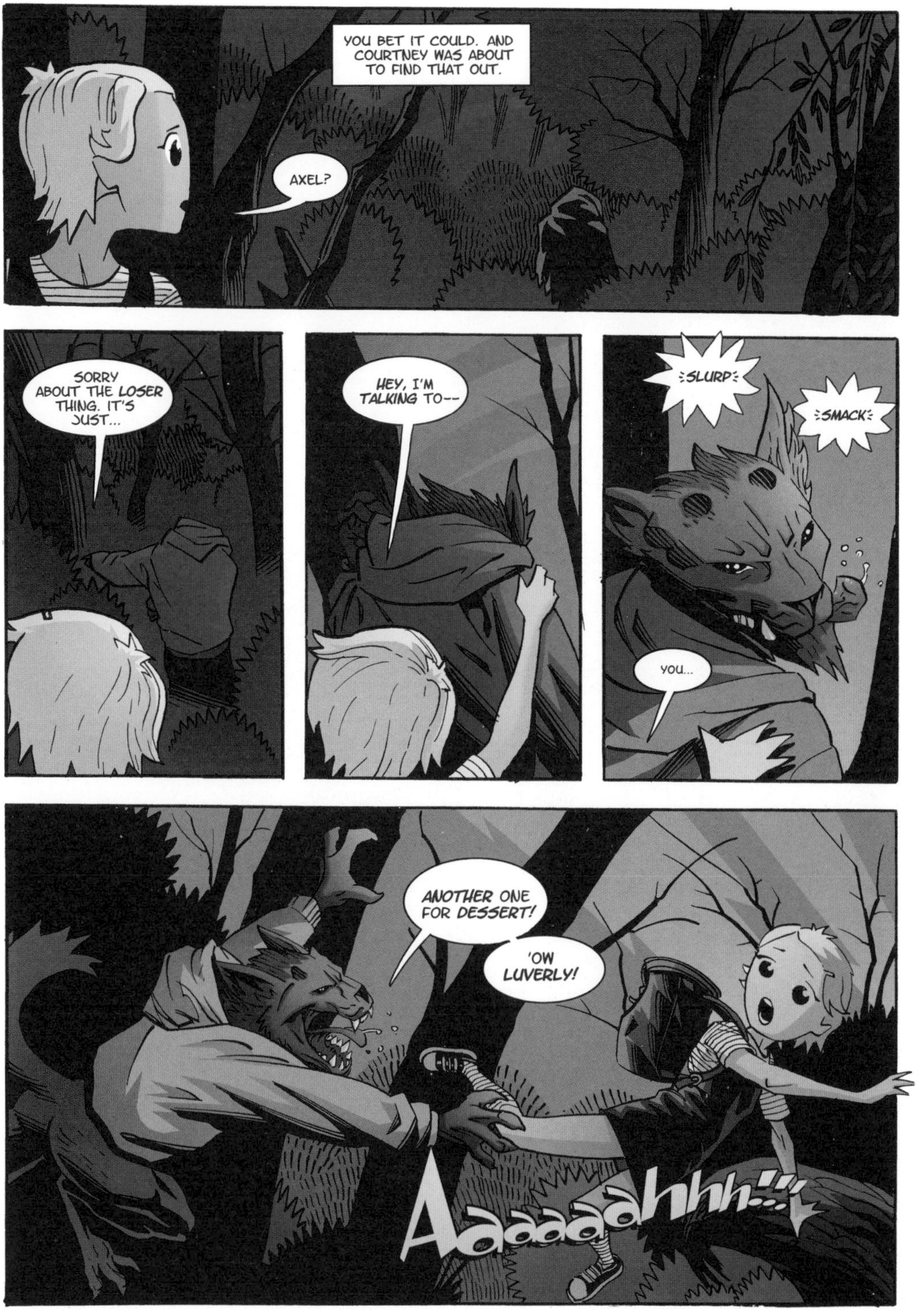
YOU BET IT COULD. AND COURTNEY WAS ABOUT TO FIND THAT OUT.
AXEL?
SORRY ABOUT THE LOSER THING. IT'S JUST...
HEY, I'M TALKING TO--
SLURP
SMACK
YOU...
ANOTHER ONE FOR DESSERT!
'OW LUVERLY!
Aaaaaahhh!!!

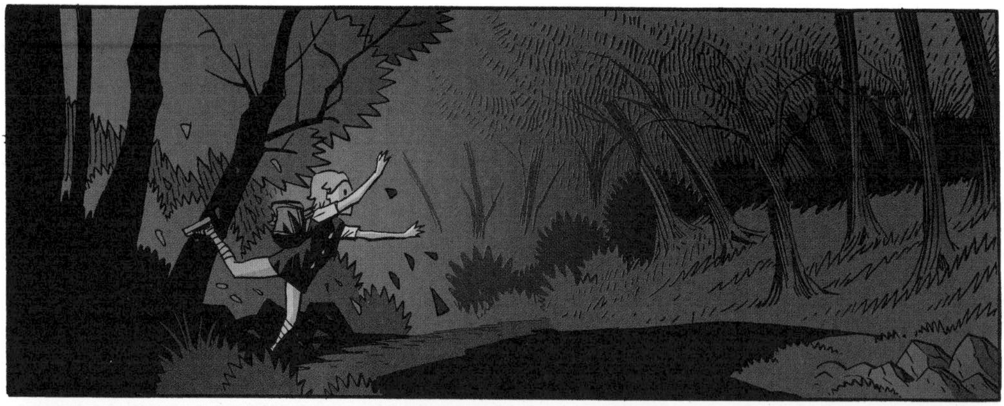

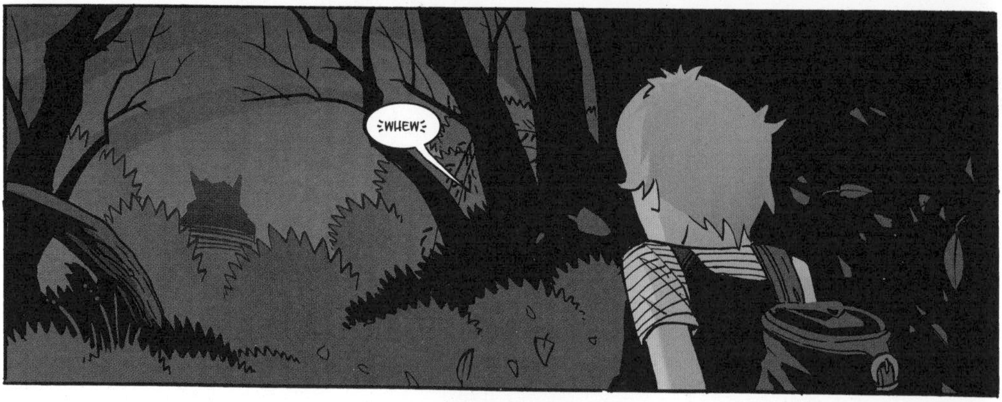
WHEW

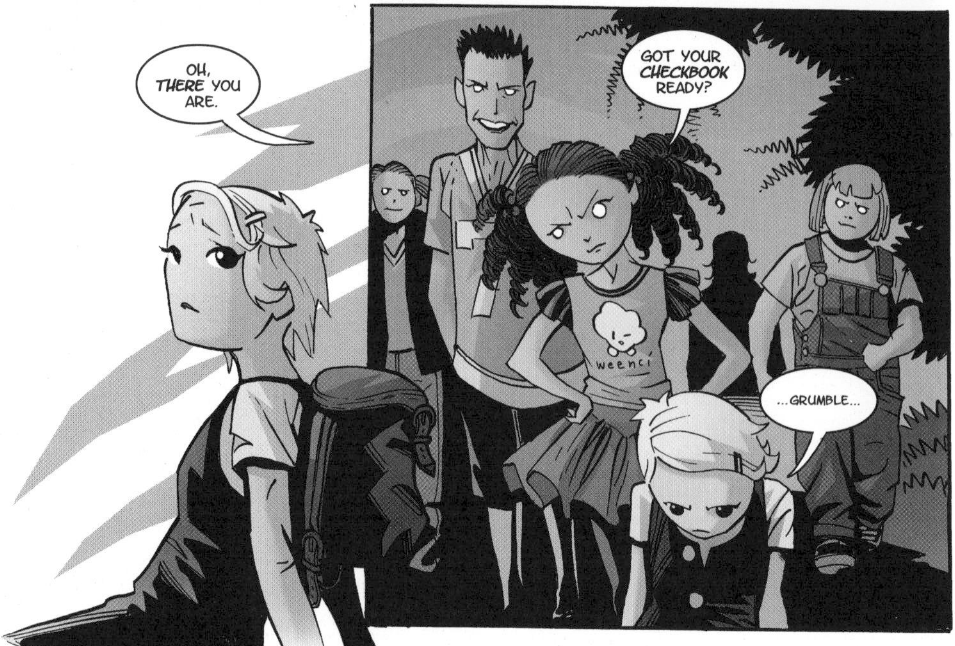
OH, THERE YOU ARE.
GOT YOUR CHECKBOOK READY?
weenci
...GRUMBLE...

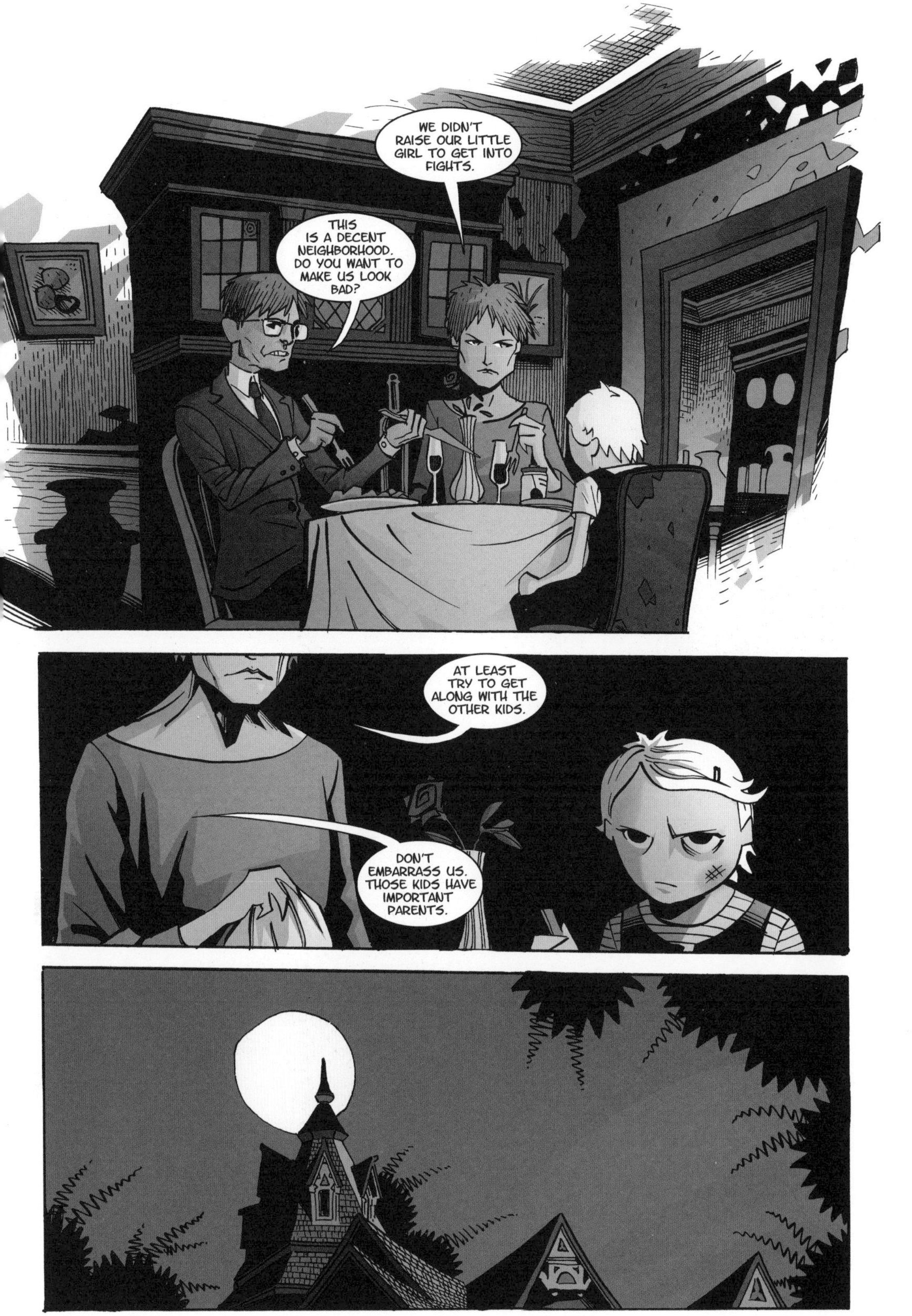
THIS IS A DECENT NEIGHBORHOOD. DO YOU WANT TO MAKE US LOOK BAD?
WE DIDN'T RAISE OUR LITTLE GIRL TO GET INTO FIGHTS.
AT LEAST TRY TO GET ALONG WITH THE OTHER KIDS.
DON'T EMBARRASS US. THOSE KIDS HAVE IMPORTANT PARENTS.

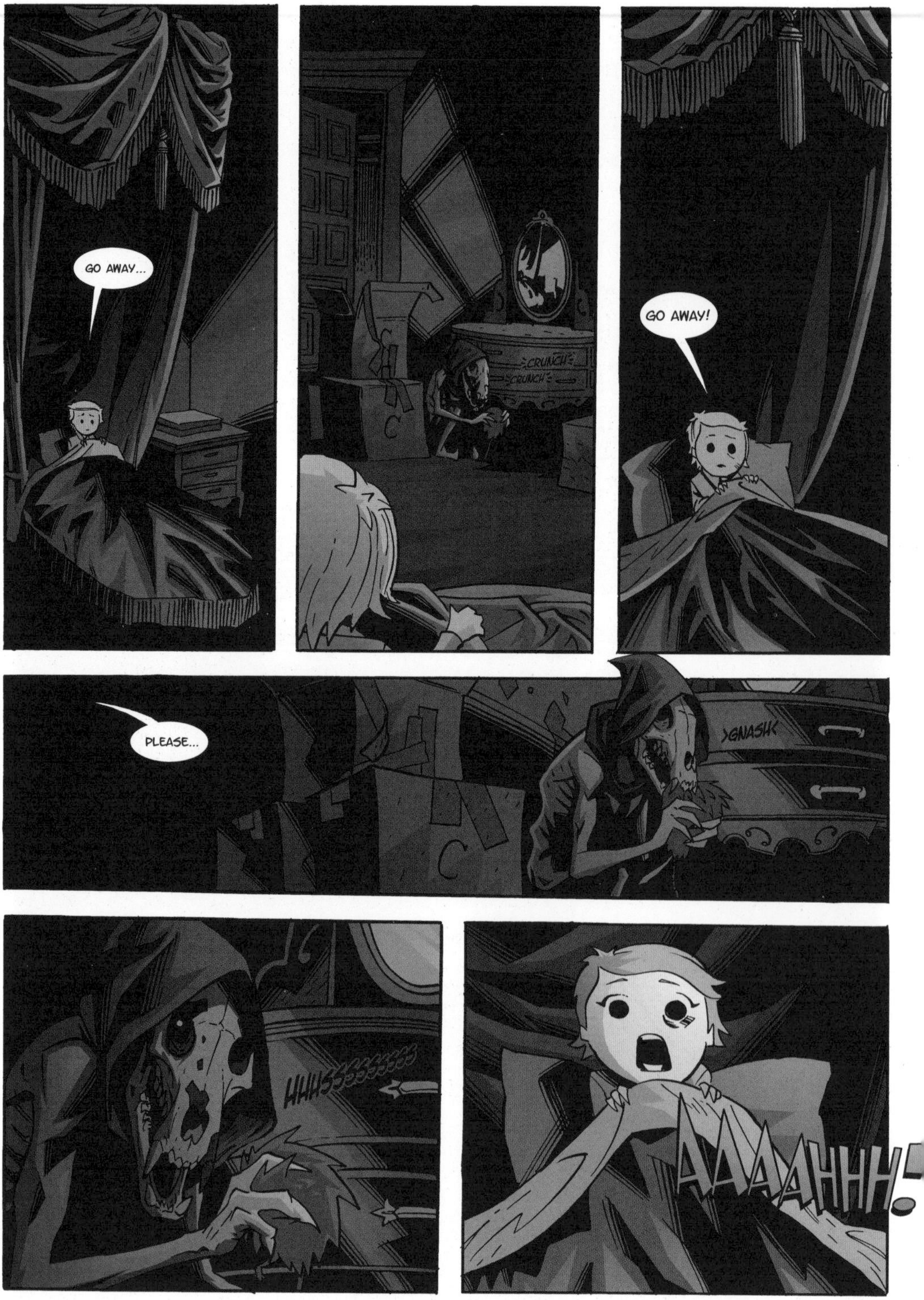
GO AWAY...
CRUNCH
CRUNCH
GO AWAY!
PLEASE...
GNASH
HHHSSSSSSSSS
AAAAHHH!

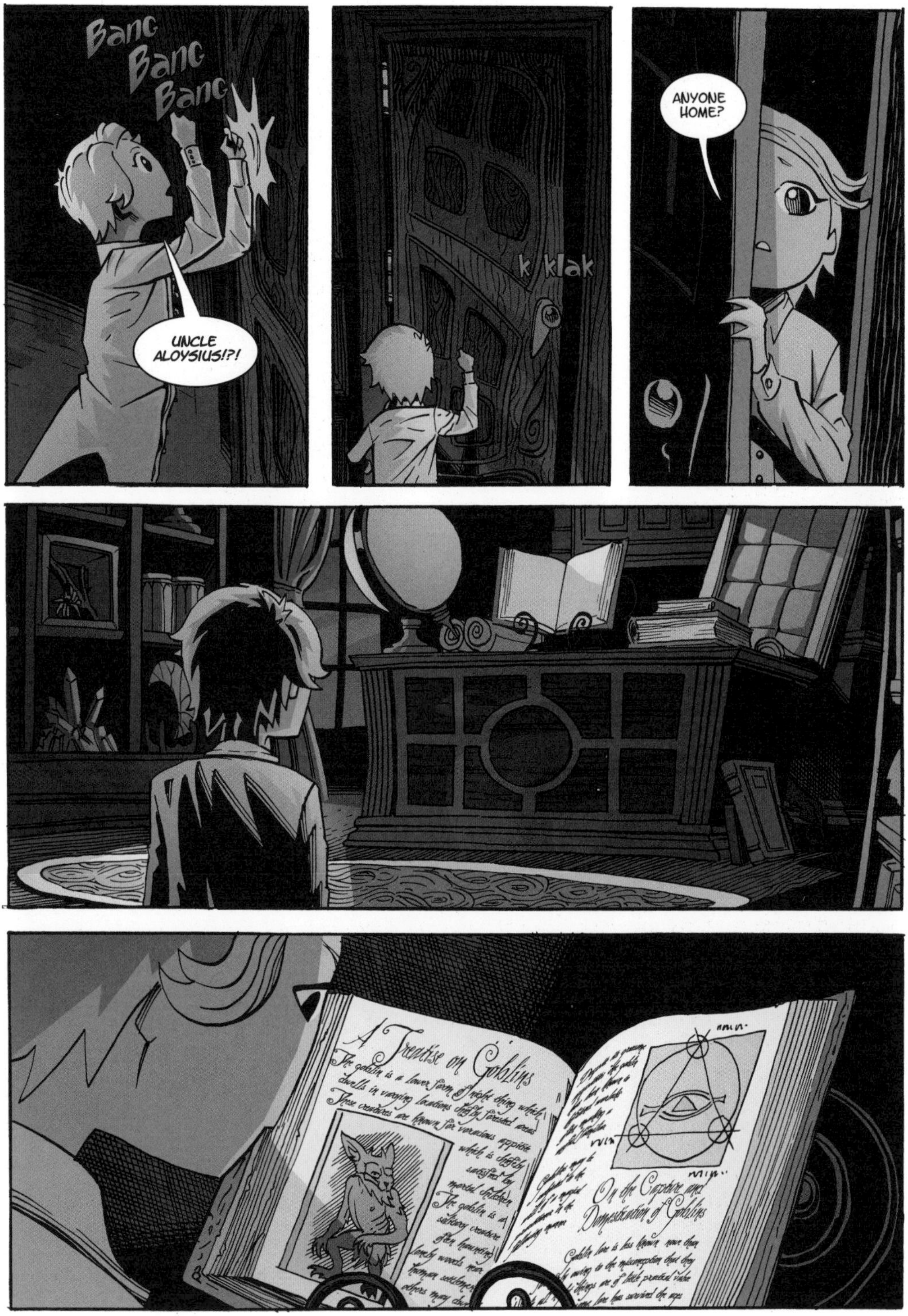
Bang
Bang
Bang
UNCLE ALOYSIUS!?!
k klak
ANYONE HOME?
A Treatise on Goblins
On the Capture and Domestication of Goblins

AXEL WAS NEVER SEEN BY ANYONE IN HILLSBOROUGH AGAIN. I'M SORRY TO SAY THAT NO ONE MISSED HIM ALL THAT MUCH.

AFTER ALL, COURTNEY HAD HER OWN PROBLEMS TO DEAL WITH.

OH, WHAT A FINE *JACKET* Y'VE GOT THERE, MR. BUTTER-WORM.

WHY *THANK'EE*, MR. BUTTERWORM. IT COME OFF A PERFEK'LY *TOOTHSOME* LITTLE FELLER.

'OW *DELIGHTFUL*, MR. BUTTERWORM. AND WHERE BE THIS LITTLE FELLER *NOW*?

BUURRRRUPP!

I COULDN'T RIGHTLY *TELL*, MR. BUTTERWORM. P'RAPS ON HIS WAY TO ME *LOWER INTESTYNES*.

EHEM!

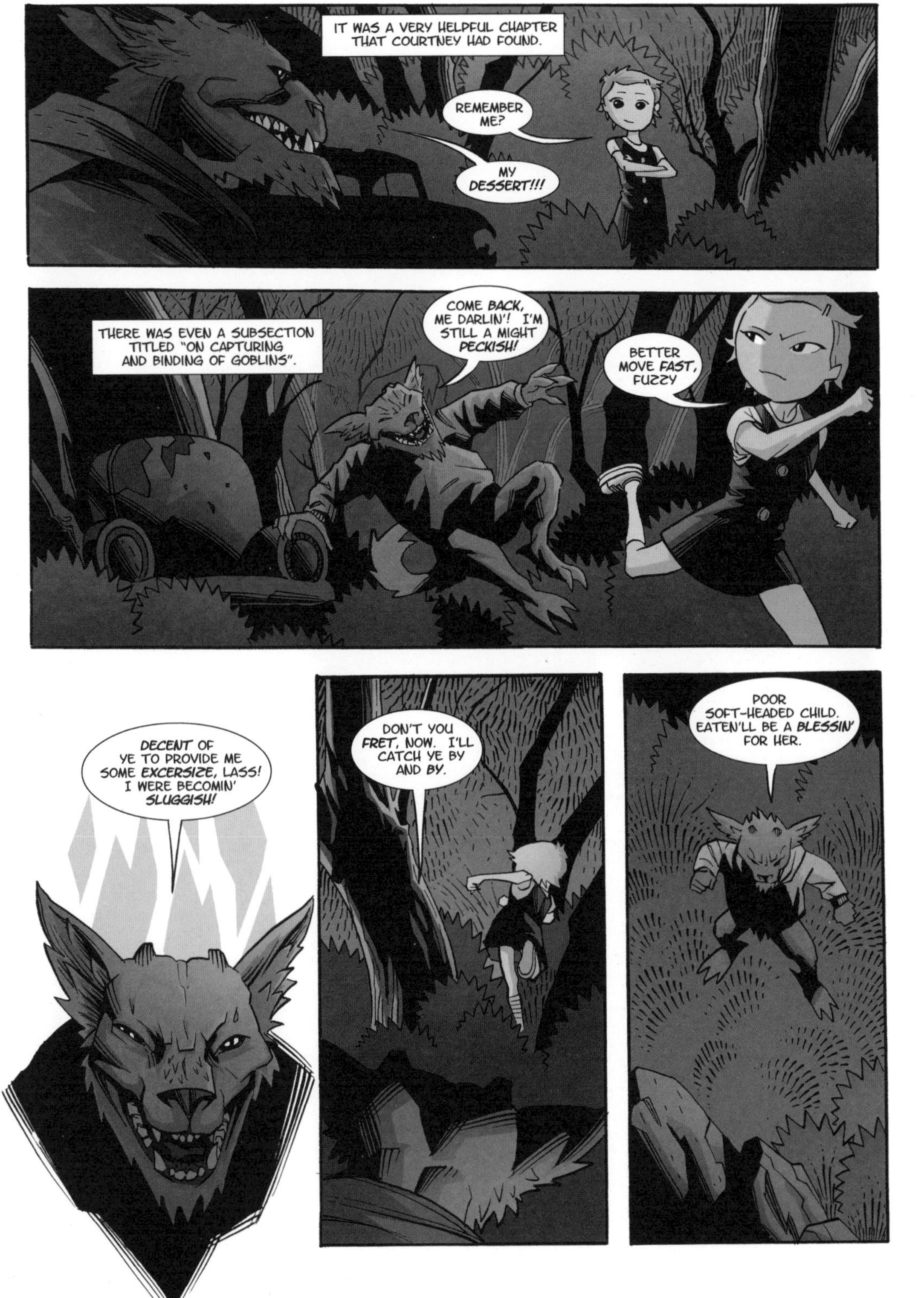
IT WAS A VERY HELPFUL CHAPTER THAT COURTNEY HAD FOUND.
REMEMBER ME?
MY DESSERT!!!
THERE WAS EVEN A SUBSECTION TITLED "ON CAPTURING AND BINDING OF GOBLINS".
COME BACK, ME DARLIN'! I'M STILL A MIGHT PECKISH!
BETTER MOVE FAST, FUZZY
DECENT OF YE TO PROVIDE ME SOME EXCERSIZE, LASS! I WERE BECOMIN' SLUGGISH!
DON'T YOU FRET, NOW. I'LL CATCH YE BY AND BY.
POOR SOFT-HEADED CHILD. EATEN'LL BE A BLESSIN' FOR HER.

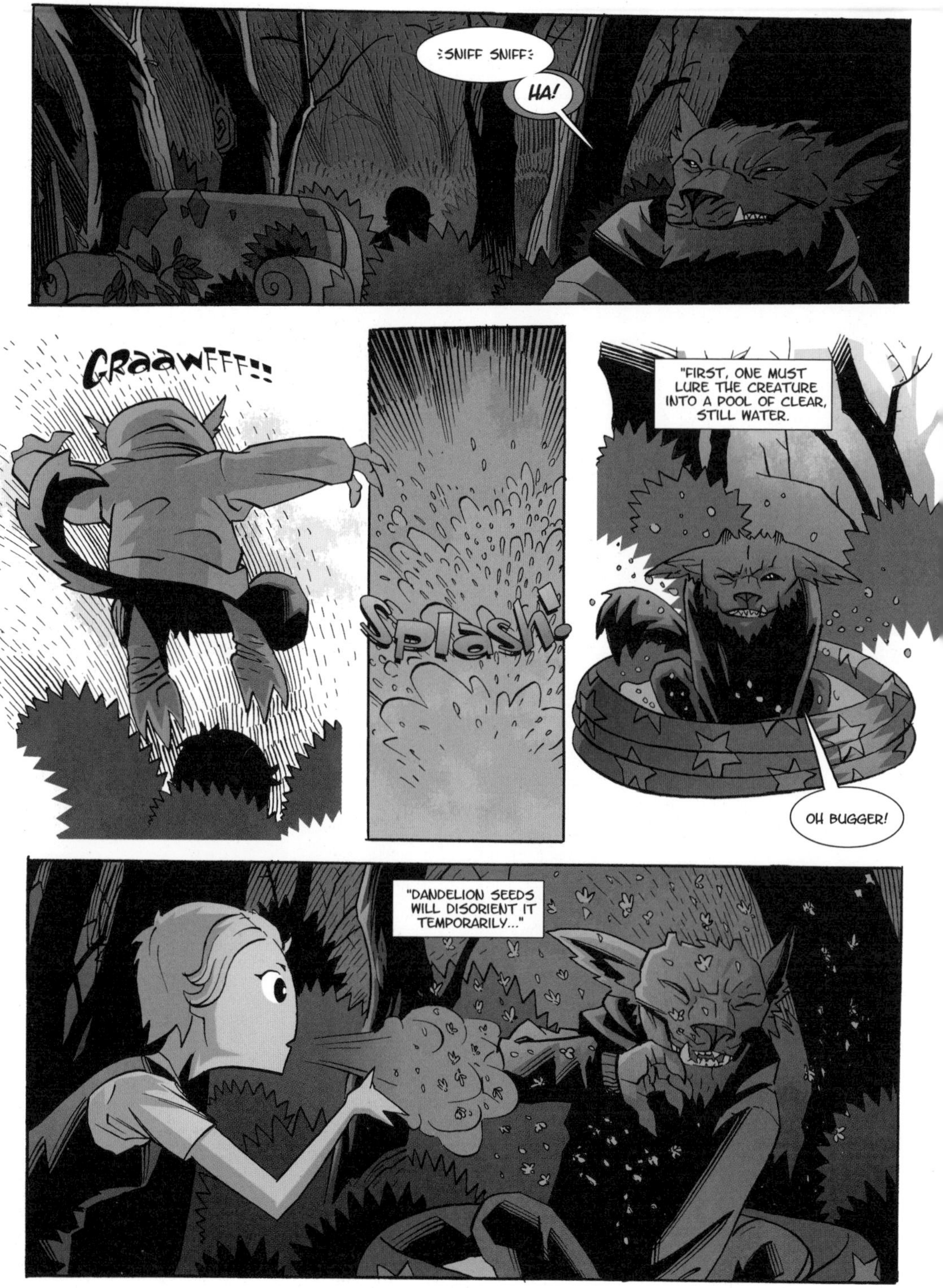
SNIFF SNIFF
HA!
GRAAWFFF!!
SPLASH!
"FIRST, ONE MUST LURE THE CREATURE INTO A POOL OF CLEAR, STILL WATER.
OH BUGGER!
"DANDELION SEEDS WILL DISORIENT IT TEMPORARILY..."

"...UNTIL YOU CAN SECURELY BIND IT IN COLD IRON."

YE JUST THINK Y'RE ALL KINDSA CLEVER, DON'T YE, MISSY?

I JUST DO MY *HOMEWORK.*

SEE YA.

YE LITTLE *MONSTER!* I'LL EAT YER FACE OFF!

LET ME OUT!

BUT THAT WASN'T THE END OF THE ESSAY.

"YOU MUST THEN WAIT FOR THREE DAYS AND THREE NIGHTS, AND RETURN AT DUSK ON THE FOURTH DAY."

Y-Y-YOU AG-GAIN...

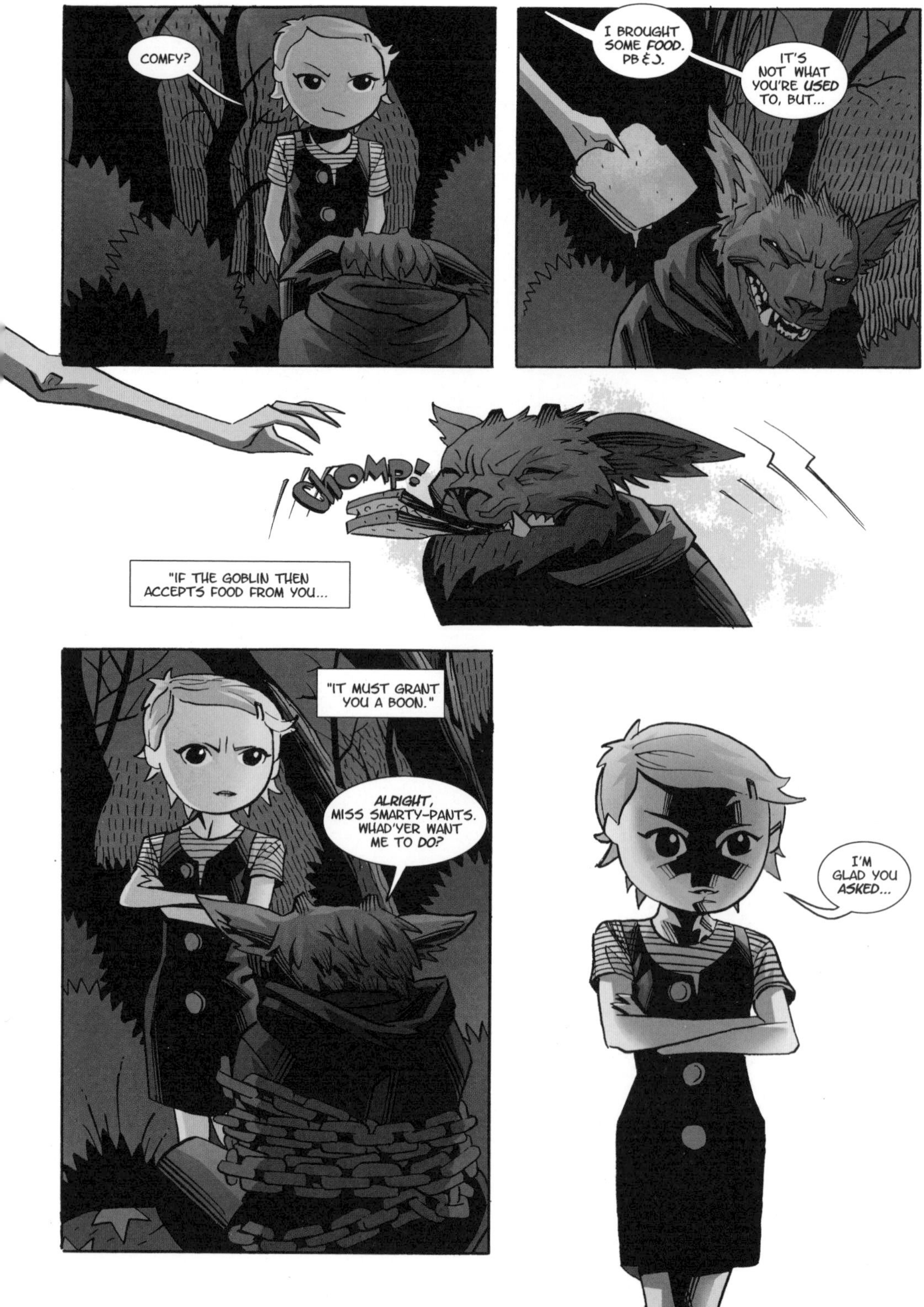
COMFY?
I BROUGHT SOME FOOD. PB & J.
IT'S NOT WHAT YOU'RE USED TO, BUT...
CHOMP!
"IF THE GOBLIN THEN ACCEPTS FOOD FROM YOU...
"IT MUST GRANT YOU A BOON."
ALRIGHT, MISS SMARTY-PANTS. WHAD'YER WANT ME TO DO?
I'M GLAD YOU ASKED...

SO I SEE YOU'VE DECIDED TO *STAY* AND MAKE THE *BEST* OF IT.

OH, IT AIN'T SO BAD HERE.

ARE YOU MAKING NEW *FRIENDS* AT SCHOOL?

I'VE MET SOME PRETTY INTERESTING PEOPLE...

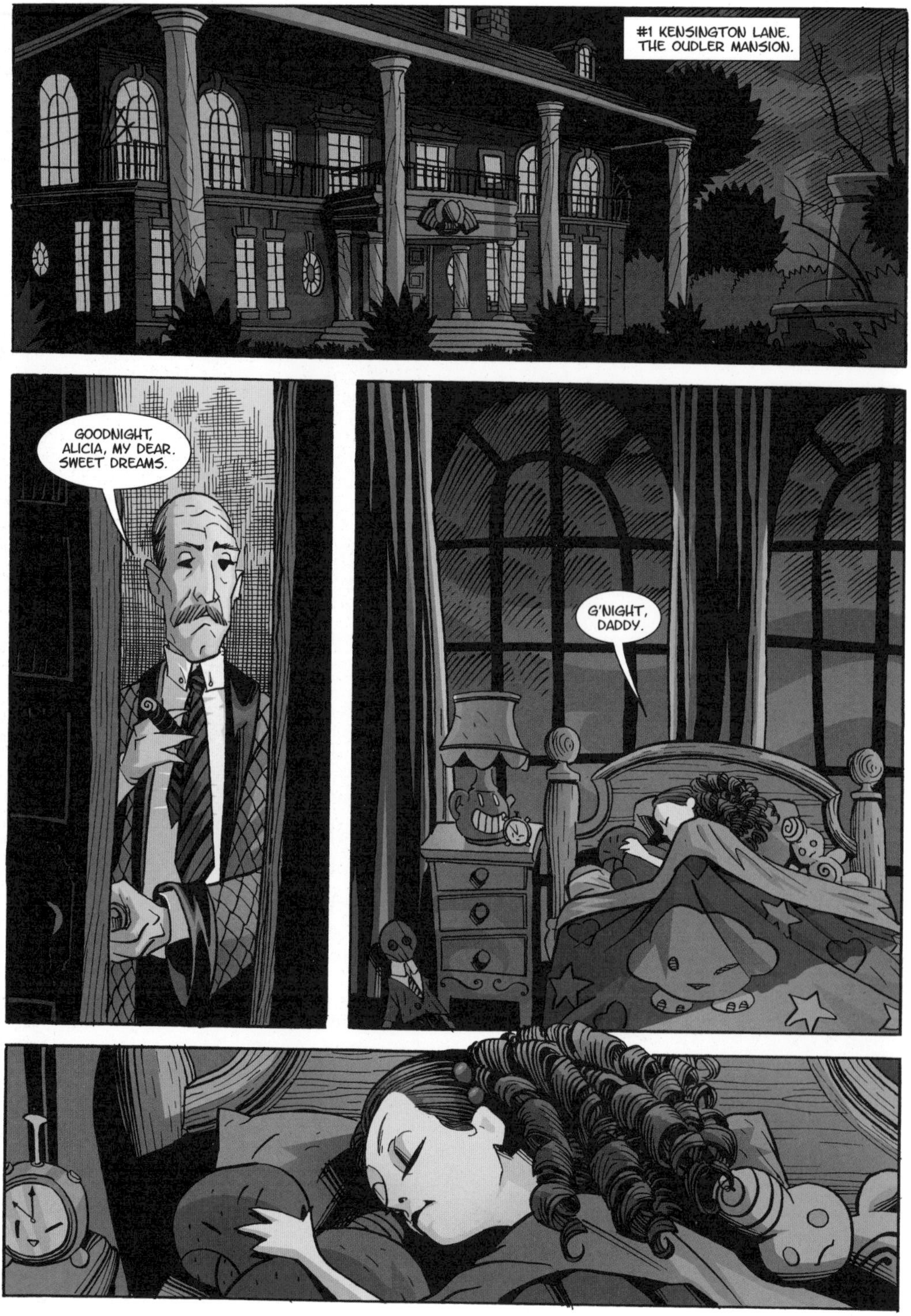
#1 KENSINGTON LANE. THE OUDLER MANSION.
GOODNIGHT, ALICIA, MY DEAR. SWEET DREAMS.
G'NIGHT, DADDY.

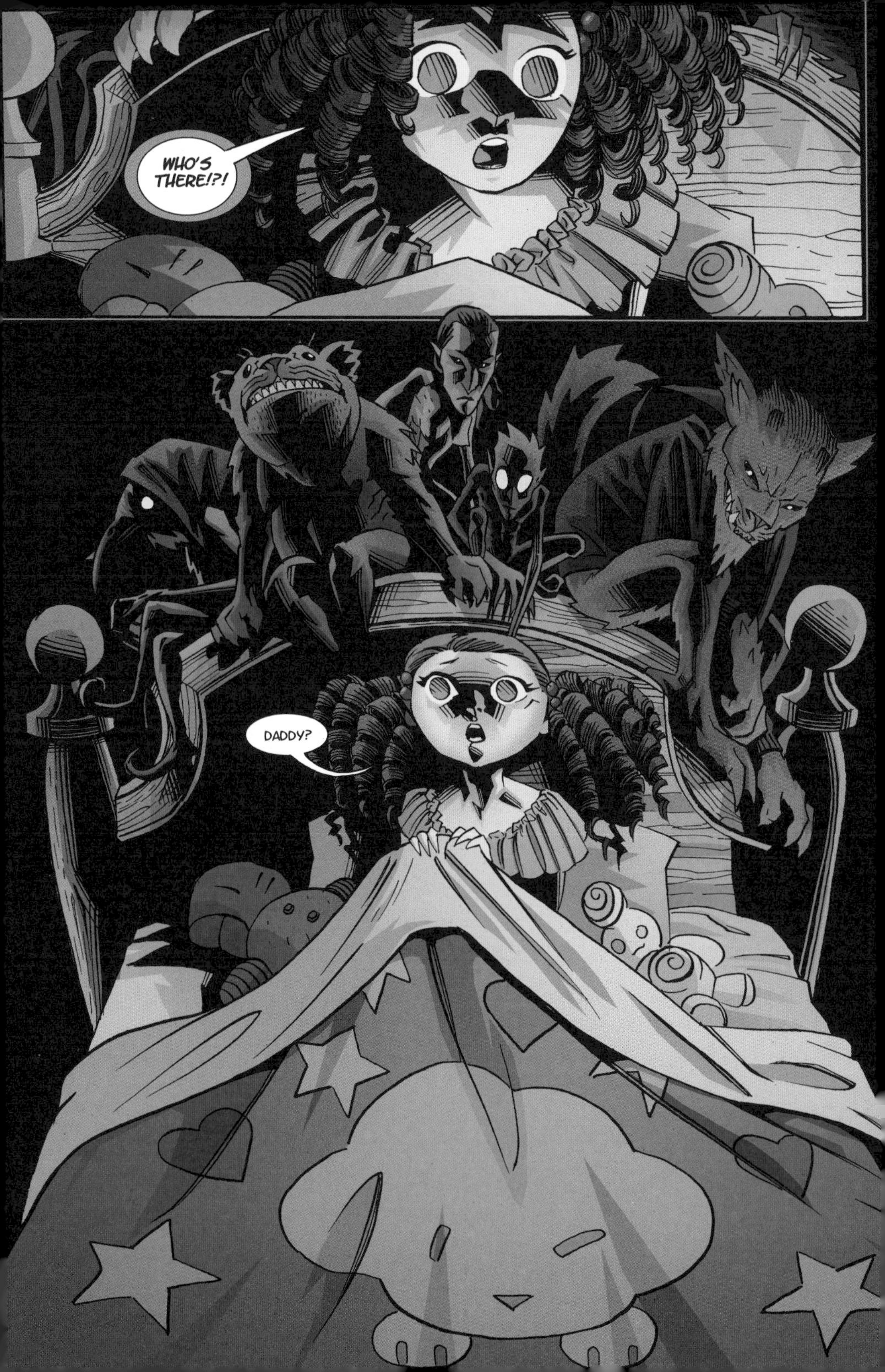
WHO'S THERE!?!
DADDY?

Chapter Two

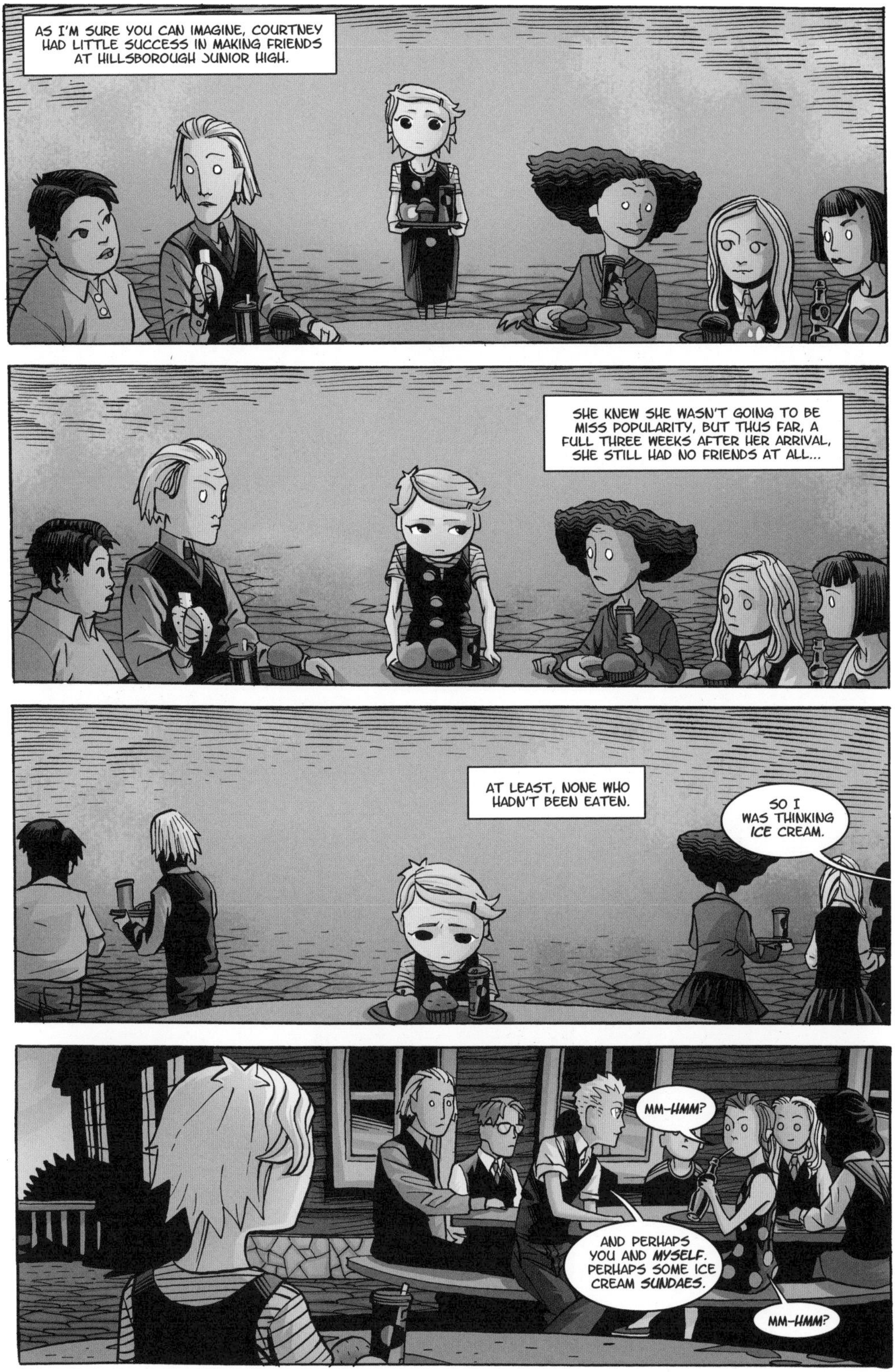
AS I'M SURE YOU CAN IMAGINE, COURTNEY HAD LITTLE SUCCESS IN MAKING FRIENDS AT HILLSBOROUGH JUNIOR HIGH.
SHE KNEW SHE WASN'T GOING TO BE MISS POPULARITY, BUT THUS FAR, A FULL THREE WEEKS AFTER HER ARRIVAL, SHE STILL HAD NO FRIENDS AT ALL...
AT LEAST, NONE WHO HADN'T BEEN EATEN.
SO I WAS THINKING ICE CREAM.
MM-HMM?
AND PERHAPS YOU AND MYSELF. PERHAPS SOME ICE CREAM SUNDAES.
MM-HMM?

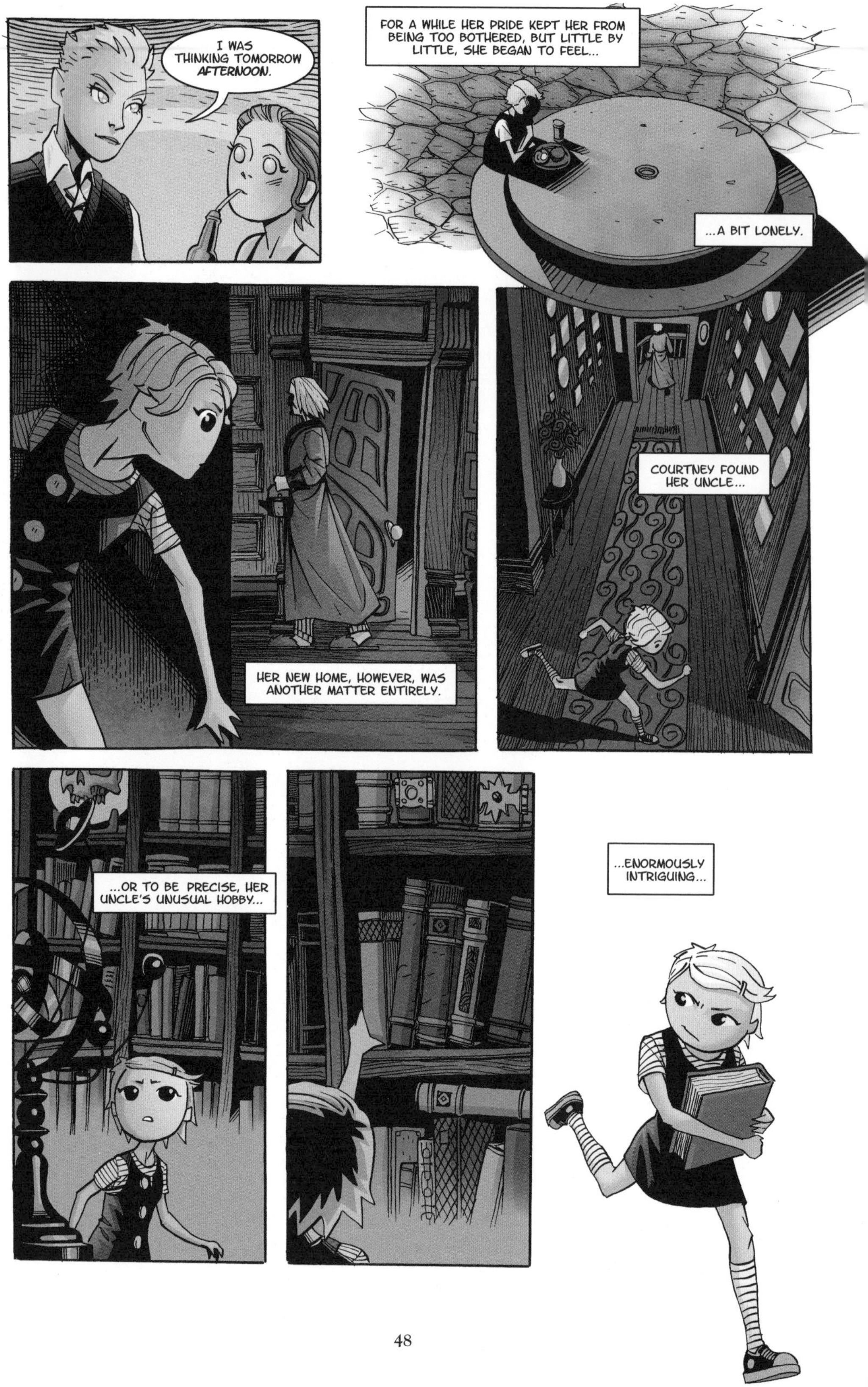
I WAS THINKING TOMORROW AFTERNOON.
FOR A WHILE HER PRIDE KEPT HER FROM BEING TOO BOTHERED, BUT LITTLE BY LITTLE, SHE BEGAN TO FEEL...
...A BIT LONELY.
HER NEW HOME, HOWEVER, WAS ANOTHER MATTER ENTIRELY.
COURTNEY FOUND HER UNCLE...
...OR TO BE PRECISE, HER UNCLE'S UNUSUAL HOBBY...
...ENORMOUSLY INTRIGUING...

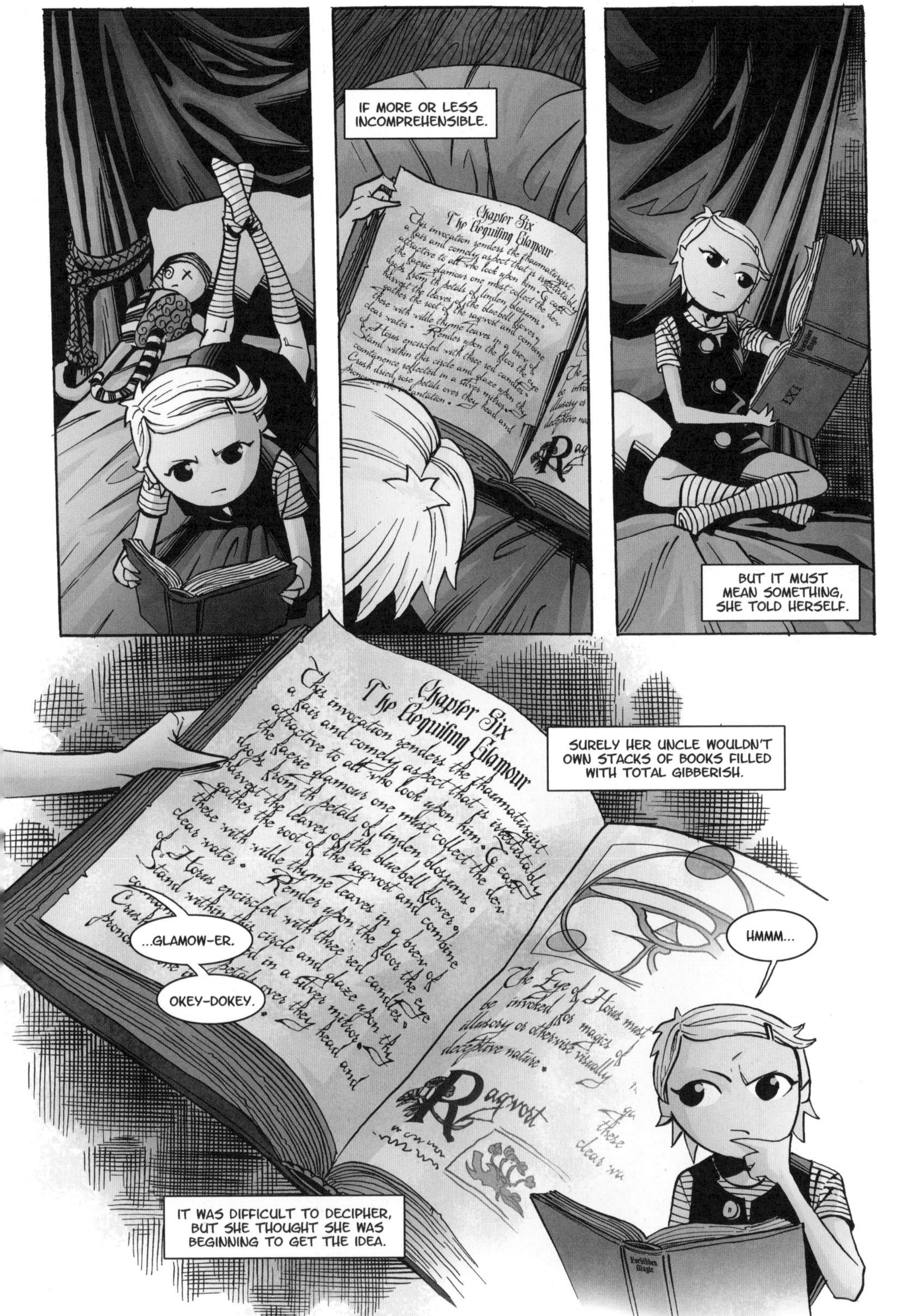
IF MORE OR LESS INCOMPREHENSIBLE.
BUT IT MUST MEAN SOMETHING, SHE TOLD HERSELF.
SURELY HER UNCLE WOULDN'T OWN STACKS OF BOOKS FILLED WITH TOTAL GIBBERISH.
...GLAMOW-ER.
OKEY-DOKEY.
HMMM...
IT WAS DIFFICULT TO DECIPHER, BUT SHE THOUGHT SHE WAS BEGINNING TO GET THE IDEA.

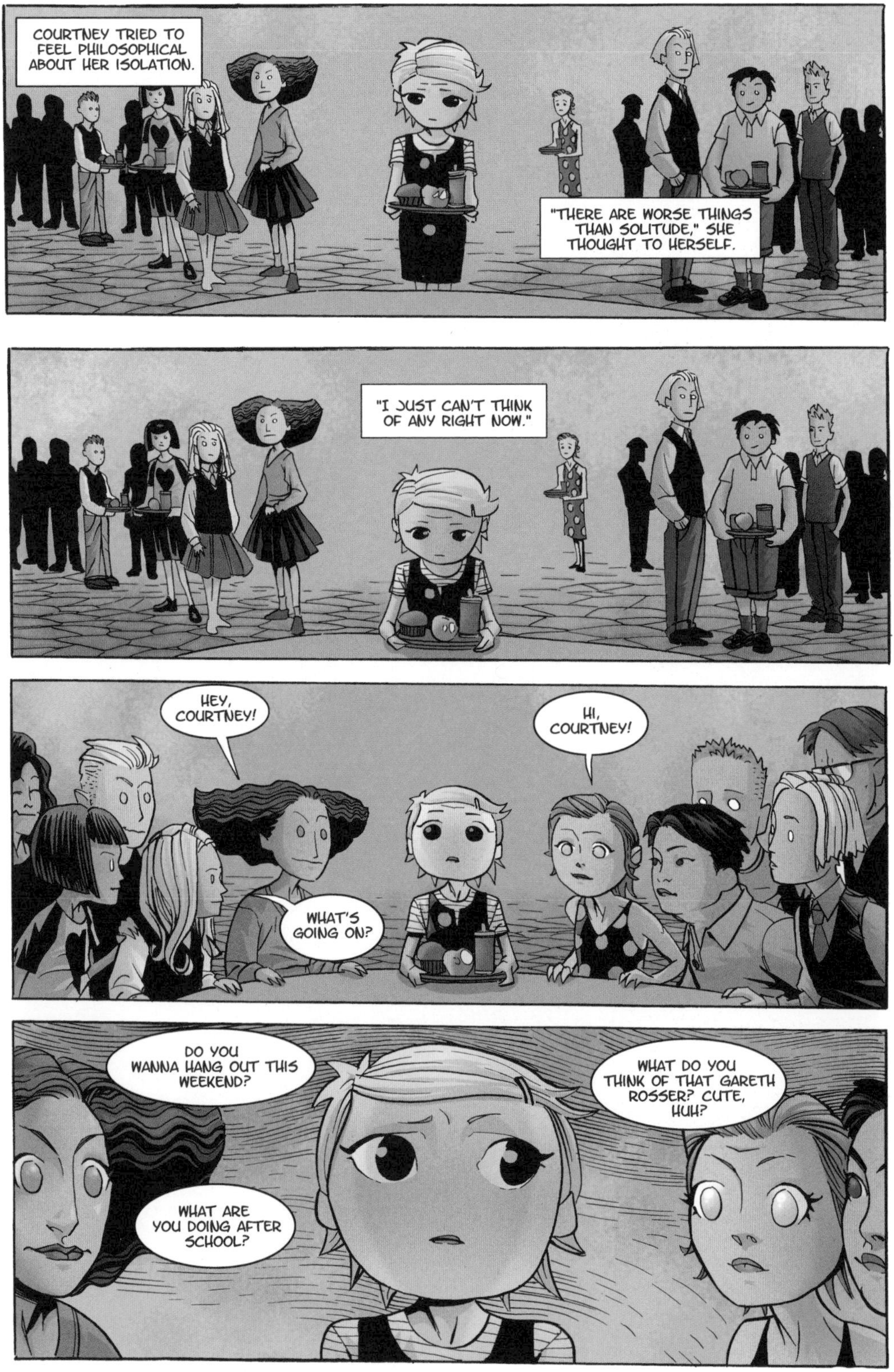
COURTNEY TRIED TO FEEL PHILOSOPHICAL ABOUT HER ISOLATION.
"THERE ARE WORSE THINGS THAN SOLITUDE," SHE THOUGHT TO HERSELF.
"I JUST CAN'T THINK OF ANY RIGHT NOW."
HEY, COURTNEY!
HI, COURTNEY!
WHAT'S GOING ON?
DO YOU WANNA HANG OUT THIS WEEKEND?
WHAT DO YOU THINK OF THAT GARETH ROSSER? CUTE, HUH?
WHAT ARE YOU DOING AFTER SCHOOL?

AND FOR THE REMAINDER OF THE DAY, COURTNEY CONTINUED TO BE THE CENTER OF ATTENTION.

Did your ancestors come over on the Mayflower?

AND *WHY* DID THE PATRIOTS ATTACK THE *SHIPMENT?*

COURTNEY?

OH, UM, BECAUSE PURITANS CAN'T HAVE *CAFFEINE?* SINFUL?

THAT'S A VERY... CREATIVE ANSWER. VERY *GOOD,* COURTNEY.

IT WAS *ALSO* BECAUSE *IMPORT* TAXES WERE EXTREMELY *HIGH,* AND THE COLONISTS FELT THEY WERE BEING *EXPLOITED...*

YEAH, GOT IT.

BUT I *LIKE* THE WAY YOUR *MIND* WORKS, YOUNG LADY.

KEEP IT *UP.*

Did your ancestors come over on the Mayflower?

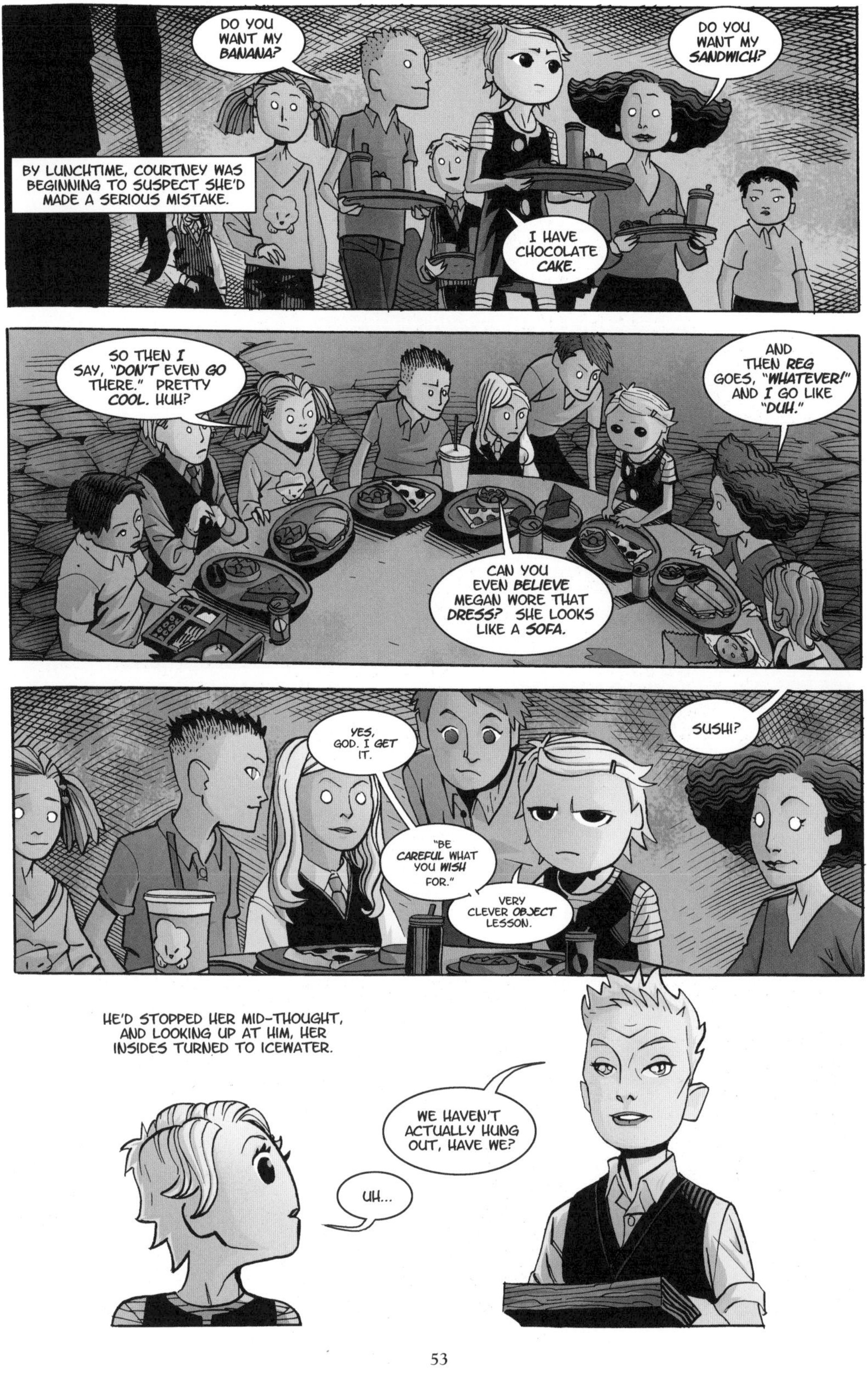
BY LUNCHTIME, COURTNEY WAS BEGINNING TO SUSPECT SHE'D MADE A SERIOUS MISTAKE.
DO YOU WANT MY BANANA?
DO YOU WANT MY SANDWICH?
I HAVE CHOCOLATE CAKE.
SO THEN I SAY, "DON'T EVEN GO THERE." PRETTY COOL. HUH?
AND THEN REG GOES, "WHATEVER!" AND I GO LIKE "DUH."
CAN YOU EVEN BELIEVE MEGAN WORE THAT DRESS? SHE LOOKS LIKE A SOFA.
YES, GOD. I GET IT.
SUSHI?
"BE CAREFUL WHAT YOU WISH FOR."
VERY CLEVER OBJECT LESSON.
HE'D STOPPED HER MID-THOUGHT, AND LOOKING UP AT HIM, HER INSIDES TURNED TO ICEWATER.
WE HAVEN'T ACTUALLY HUNG OUT, HAVE WE?
UH...

COURTNEY CAREFULLY AVOIDED BOYS LIKE GARETH FOR EXACTLY THIS REASON. THEY MADE HER FEEL STRANGE IN WAYS THAT SHE DIDN'T QUITE UNDERSTAND.

BUT YOU *DEFINITELY* SEEM LIKE YOU'RE WORTH HANGING *OUT* WITH.

UH...

THANKS...

I WAS THINKING *ICE CREAM*. I KNOW THIS *PLACE*. IT'S PRETTY *COOL*.

SH--... SURE... COOL. I LIKE...

COOL.

MAYBE THIS SPELL CASTING WASN'T SUCH A BAD IDEA AFTER ALL.

GREAT.

SEE YOU AFTER *SCHOOL*.

OKAY.

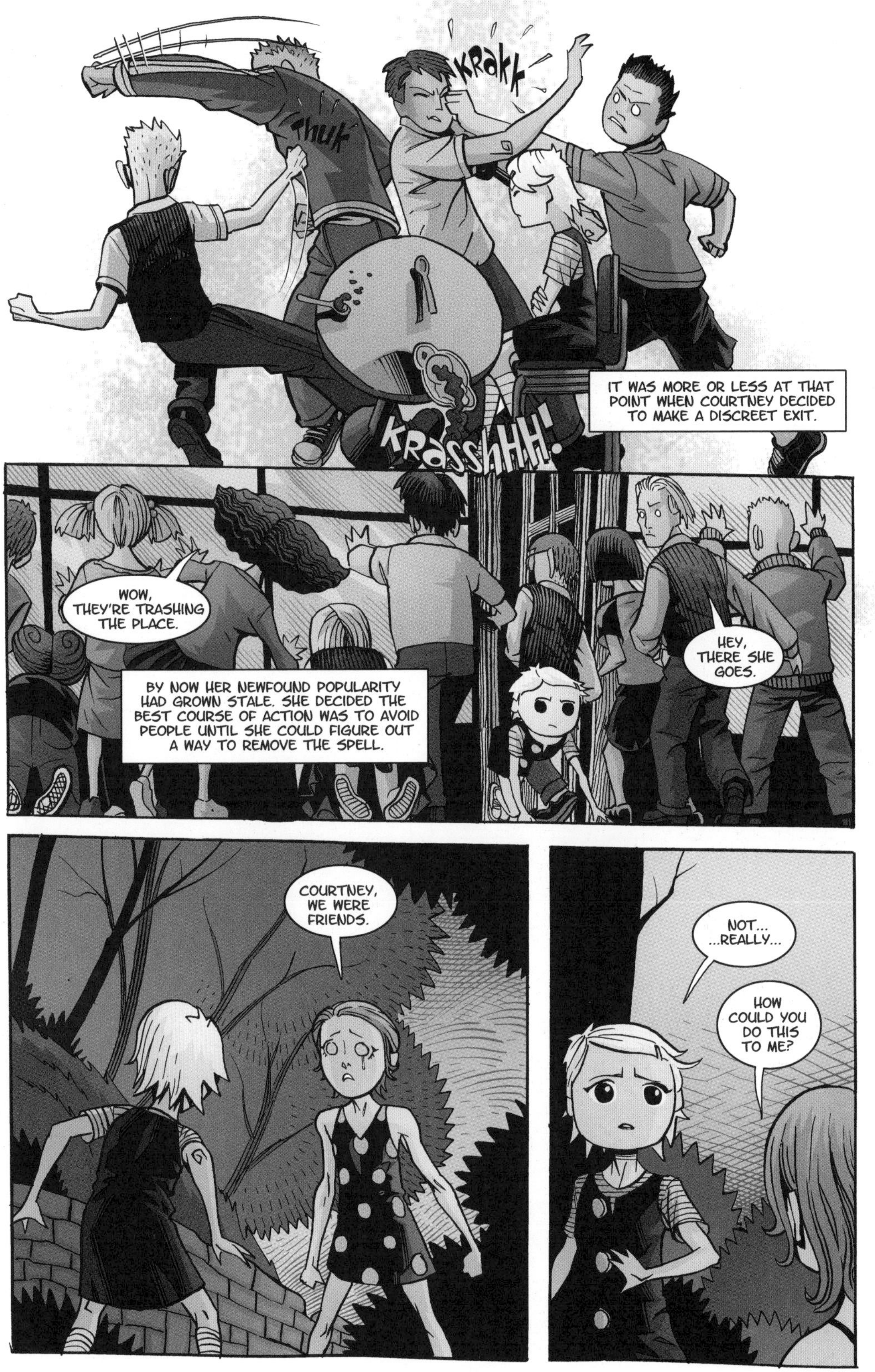
THUK
KRAKK
KRASSHHH!
IT WAS MORE OR LESS AT THAT POINT WHEN COURTNEY DECIDED TO MAKE A DISCREET EXIT.
WOW, THEY'RE TRASHING THE PLACE.
BY NOW HER NEWFOUND POPULARITY HAD GROWN STALE. SHE DECIDED THE BEST COURSE OF ACTION WAS TO AVOID PEOPLE UNTIL SHE COULD FIGURE OUT A WAY TO REMOVE THE SPELL.
HEY, THERE SHE GOES.
COURTNEY, WE WERE FRIENDS.
NOT... ...REALLY...
HOW COULD YOU DO THIS TO ME?

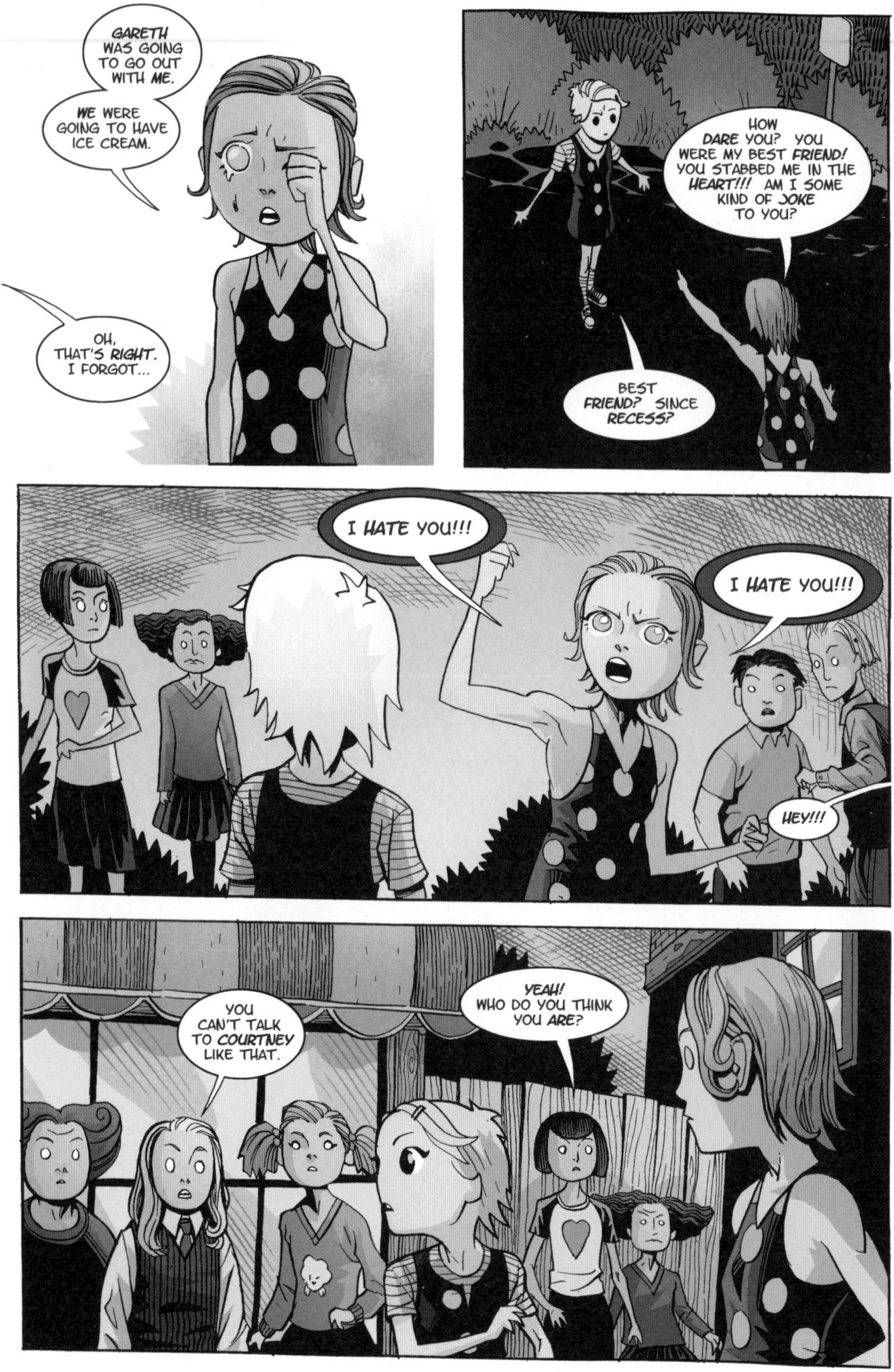
GARETH WAS GOING TO GO OUT WITH ME.
WE WERE GOING TO HAVE ICE CREAM.
OH, THAT'S RIGHT. I FORGOT...
HOW DARE YOU? YOU WERE MY BEST FRIEND! YOU STABBED ME IN THE HEART!!! AM I SOME KIND OF JOKE TO YOU?
BEST FRIEND? SINCE RECESS?
I HATE YOU!!!
I HATE YOU!!!
HEY!!!
YOU CAN'T TALK TO COURTNEY LIKE THAT.
YEAH! WHO DO YOU THINK YOU ARE?

THINGS WEREN'T LOOKING GOOD FOR CATHY. COURTNEY OPTED NOT TO STAY AND WATCH.

LEAVE ME ALONE!!!

AT HOME, THINGS WERE JUST AS UNSETTLING. COURTNEY WAS DEEPLY DISTURBED TO REALIZE THAT HER PARENTS' ADORATION WAS EVEN LESS PLEASANT THAN THEIR INDIFFERENCE.

HOW'S MY LITTLE *ANGEL* TODAY?

I *HEARD* YOU'VE BEEN SPENDING TIME WITH GARETH *ROSSER'S* KID. THAT'S MY GIRL.

YOU ACTUALLY LOOK *NICE* TODAY. ARE YOU DOING SOMETHING WITH YOUR *HAIR* FOR A CHANGE?

BY CONTRAST, UNCLE ALOYSIUS SEEMED THE SAME AS EVER.

MAYBE NOT QUITE THE SAME.

PERHAPS THIS WAS HIS WAY OF EXPRESSING INTEREST.

Bone
Bone

COULD *TONIGHT* POSSIBLY GET ANY MORE *UNCOMFORTABLE*?

ASK A SILLY QUESTION...

YEAH, SO WE NEED TO *TALK*.

SURE. WE'LL DO *LUNCH* SOMETIME.

Ka'klak

BONG
BONG
BONG
BONG
BONG
BONG
BONG
BONG
BONG
BONG
BONG
BONG

FOR *CRYIN'* OUT LOUD!

I'M IN LOVE WITH YOU.

OW!!!

KRUNCH

I CAN STAND HERE RINGING THE DOORBELL ALL NIGHT.

WHO *IS* IT, SWEETHEART?

IS IT *HOOLIGANS?*

IS IT GARETH *JUNIOR?*

FINE! OUTSIDE.

WE'LL TALK OUTSIDE.

I FOUND THESE IN YOUR ROOM.

I'M VERY SORRY, SIR.

I UNDERSTAND YOUR *CURIOSITY*.

AND I *IMAGINE* YOU'VE NOTICED HOW *DANGEROUS* SUCH POWER CAN BE.

OH YEAH.

YOU'RE *LUCKY*. YOU SAW ONLY THE *TIP* OF THE *ICEBERG*.

IT COULD HAVE BEEN *MUCH* WORSE.

IT WAS GETTING PRETTY *BAD* FOR A WHILE.

YOU DID DRAW *ATTENTION* TO YOURSELF, SOMETHING AN *INTELLIGENT* WITCH TRIES TO *AVOID*.

WITCH?

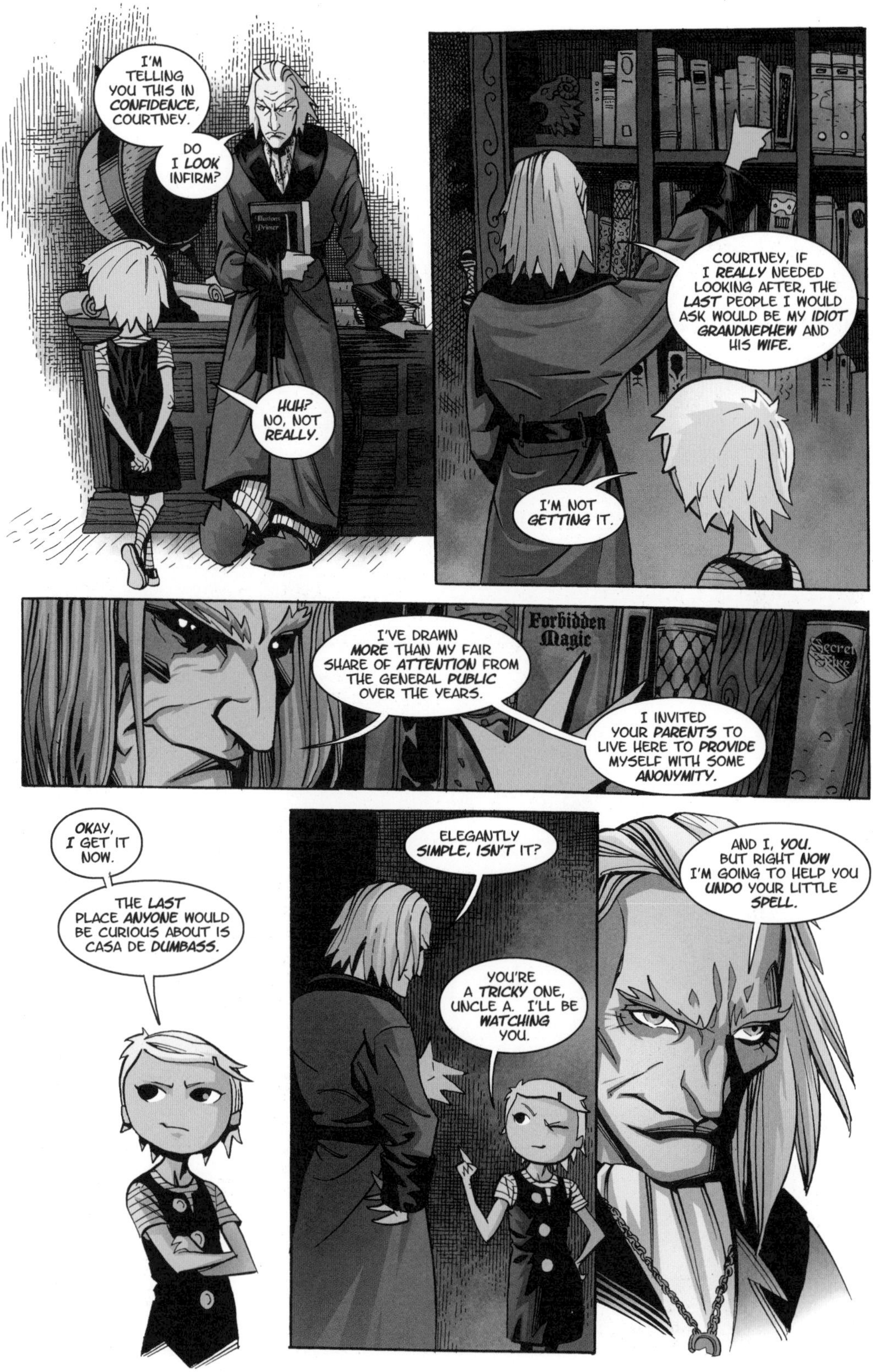
I'M TELLING YOU THIS IN CONFIDENCE, COURTNEY.
DO I LOOK INFIRM?
Illusions Primer
HUH? NO, NOT REALLY.
COURTNEY, IF I REALLY NEEDED LOOKING AFTER, THE LAST PEOPLE I WOULD ASK WOULD BE MY IDIOT GRANDNEPHEW AND HIS WIFE.
I'M NOT GETTING IT.
Forbidden Magic
I'VE DRAWN MORE THAN MY FAIR SHARE OF ATTENTION FROM THE GENERAL PUBLIC OVER THE YEARS.
I INVITED YOUR PARENTS TO LIVE HERE TO PROVIDE MYSELF WITH SOME ANONYMITY.
OKAY, I GET IT NOW.
THE LAST PLACE ANYONE WOULD BE CURIOUS ABOUT IS CASA DE DUMBASS.
ELEGANTLY SIMPLE, ISN'T IT?
YOU'RE A TRICKY ONE, UNCLE A. I'LL BE WATCHING YOU.
AND I, YOU. BUT RIGHT NOW I'M GOING TO HELP YOU UNDO YOUR LITTLE SPELL.

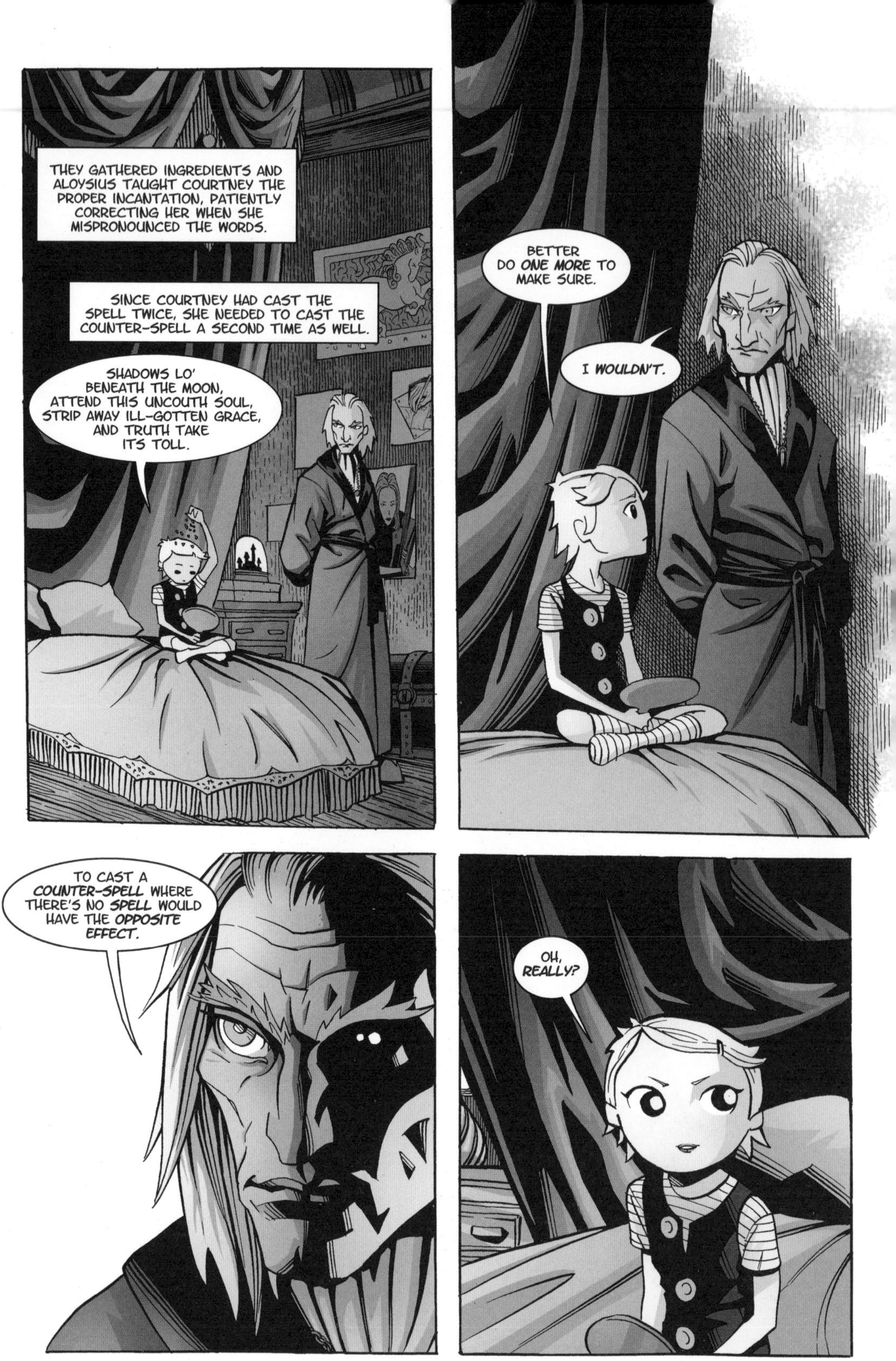
THEY GATHERED INGREDIENTS AND ALOYSIUS TAUGHT COURTNEY THE PROPER INCANTATION, PATIENTLY CORRECTING HER WHEN SHE MISPRONOUNCED THE WORDS.
SINCE COURTNEY HAD CAST THE SPELL TWICE, SHE NEEDED TO CAST THE COUNTER-SPELL A SECOND TIME AS WELL.
SHADOWS LO' BENEATH THE MOON, ATTEND THIS UNCOUTH SOUL, STRIP AWAY ILL-GOTTEN GRACE, AND TRUTH TAKE ITS TOLL.
BETTER DO ONE MORE TO MAKE SURE.
I WOULDN'T.
TO CAST A COUNTER-SPELL WHERE THERE'S NO SPELL WOULD HAVE THE OPPOSITE EFFECT.
OH, REALLY?

AAAHH...

SO YEAH, COURTNEY. I WAS THINKING...

YOU WEREN'T GOING TO *MENTION*... LAST *NIGHT*... OR... ANYTHING THAT *HAPPENED*... TO ANYONE. WERE *YOU*?

HADN'T REALLY *THOUGHT* ABOUT IT.

WELL IT'S *JUST* THAT, YOU KNOW, IT WOULD PROBABLY BE *BETTER* IF YOU DIDN'T *MENTION* IT.

IT *MIGHT* MAKE... US BOTH... ...LOOK BAD.

MOSTLY YOU. I'M JUST THINKING OF YOUR *REPUTATION.*

GEE. THANKS.

70

Chapter Three

THE WHOLE MESS ESSENTIALLY BEGAN OVER DRINKS AT THE HILLSBOROUGH MIDDLE SCHOOL PARENTS' SOCIAL.

HILLSBOROUGH MIDDLE SCHOOL

THIS WAS A CAREFULLY ORCHESTRATED MANEUVER OF THE SORT THAT MRS. CRUMRIN WAS WELL PRACTICED.

WATCH CLOSELY...

EVELYN DEAR...

I'VE *HEARD* YOU'VE HAD *TROUBLE* FINDING ADEQUATE *CHILDCARE*.

WHAT A DISASTER.

YOU'D *THINK* MAYOR *TATE* WOULD HAVE A BETTER BEHAVED *DAUGHTER*.

SHE *SEEMED* POLITE ENOUGH AT *FIRST*.

BUT *HONESTLY!* WHO KNEW THAT *TEENAGERS* COULD CAUSE SUCH DAMAGE?

THEY'D TURNED THE *HOUSE* INTO A *DISCO.*

THERE WERE SIX OR *SEVEN* OF THEM, PLAYING THAT *LOUD THUMPY MUSIC.* THE CARPET IS BEYOND HELP.

OH *HONEY...*

ADD TO *THAT* SIX BOTTLES OF *ROERDERER.* CAN YOU *IMAGINE?*

HOW *AWFUL.*

AND *SEVERAL HUNDRED DOLLARS* IN *LONG DISTANCE* BILLS TO SOME *YOUTH* HOSTEL IN *AMSTERDAM.*

YOU *POOR—*

OH! WHAT A *SHAME.*

ISN'T ROERDERER A *THOUSAND DOLLARS* A BOTTLE?

YOU POOR *DEAR.*

YOU *KNOW,* IF YOU'RE STILL IN THE MARKET FOR A *SITTER...*

SUBTLE, ISN'T SHE?

JEBEDIAH FINCH, IN ADDITION TO BEING THE DISTRICT ATTORNEY FOR THE WHOLE COUNTY, CAME FROM OLD MONEY.

HE AND HIS WIFE WERE SOME OF THE MOST RESPECTED MEMBERS OF THE COMMUNITY...

AND ANY FRIENDS OF THEIRS WERE, BY PROXY, ALSO HIGHLY RESPECTABLE.

ISN'T SHE A LITTLE *YOUNG?*

MAYBE, BUT LOOK AT IT *THIS WAY.*

OF ALL THE GIRLS IN THE *NEIGHBORHOOD,* COURTNEY *CRUMRIN* IS THE *LEAST* LIKELY TO THROW A WILD PARTY.

HEH HEH, OR RUN UP *PHONE* BILLS.

AND I *LOCKED* THE *LIQUOR* CABINET, JUST IN CASE.

IT'S FUNNY. WHEN I WAS A *KID*, WE ALL LIVED IN MORTAL *TERROR* OF THE CRUMRIN HOUSE.

I WOULD NEVER HAVE *IMAGINED* THAT THE OCCUPANTS WOULD BE SO...

I DON'T *KNOW*...

I THINK THE WORD YOU'RE *LOOKING* FOR IS "BANAL."

HEH...

THEY DON'T *EXACTLY* RADIATE *MYSTERY* AND *TERROR*, DO THEY?

HEH, A REAL... *CHAMP*... JEB.

HE'S...

JUST...

ADORABLE...

HE'LL BE ONE HECK OF A *QUARTERBACK* SOME DAY. GOOD STRONG *KICK* ON THE BOY.

THAT IS ONE *BUTT-UGLY* BABY.

SHHH!

...BLEARGH...

GREAT. THANKS. WELL, THAT'S IT, I THINK. LET'S GET *GOING*, DEAR.

COURTNEY, NOW DON'T LET *BOO* INTO THE ROOM.

I DON'T WANT HIM FALLING *ASLEEP* ON ROGER'S LITTLE *HEAD* AGAIN.

YOU HEAR THAT, HONEY?

SO *ANYWAY* EVELYN, WHO DO WE HAVE TO *KILL* TO GET *INVITED* TO MAYOR TATE'S *FUNDRAISER* NEXT MONTH?

...GRUMBLE...

SWEETY, DON'T BE *WEIRD.*

THIS IS MORE OR LESS HOW COURTNEY ENDED UP BABY-SITTING THE FINCHES' NEWBORN.

COURTNEY DIDN'T LIKE BABIES AT THE BEST OF TIMES. AS FAR AS SHE WAS CONCERNED, ANYTHING THAT EXISTED SOLELY TO EMIT DROOL, VOMIT, GHASTLY ODORS, AND LOUD, ANNOYING SCREAMS WAS MORE TROUBLE THAN IT WAS WORTH.

NEEDLESS TO SAY, HER PARENTS HADN'T BOTHERED TO CONSULT HER IN THE MATTER.

THE ONLY UPSIDE WAS THE FINCHES' SATELLITE DISH.

YOU'RE WATCHING THE FAMILY *LEARNING* CHANNEL.

AND *NOW,* ANGRY *TICKS* FIRE OUT OF MY *NIPPLES.*

WHAT THE...?

≋BRRR≋

ONE CREEPY BABY...

BET HE GROWS UP TO BE A DIVORCE ATTORNEY.

ALL RIGHT!

WHAT THE HECK IS GOING ON IN HERE?

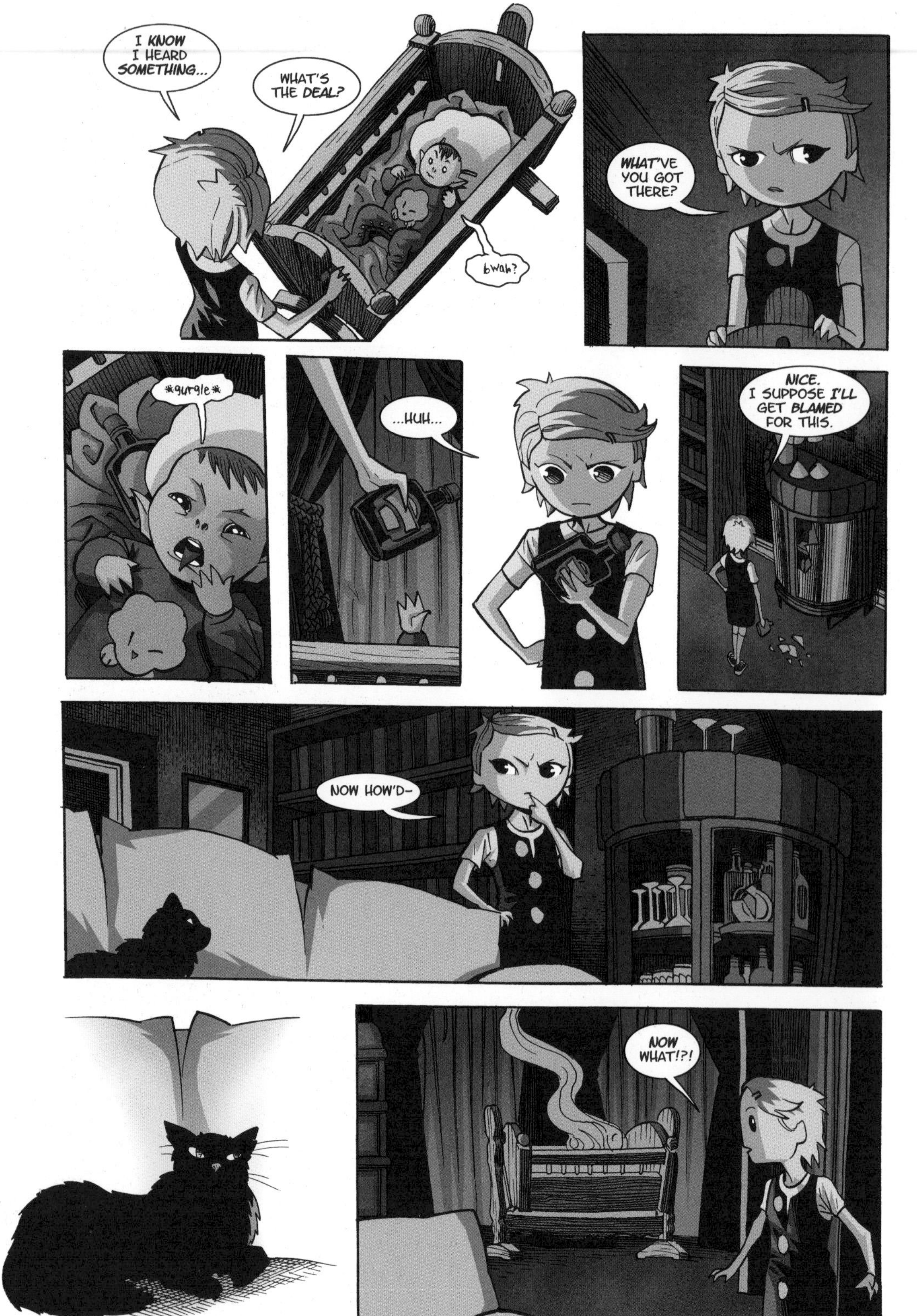
I KNOW I HEARD SOMETHING...
WHAT'S THE DEAL?
bwah?
WHAT'VE YOU GOT THERE?
gurgle
...HUH...
NICE. I SUPPOSE I'LL GET BLAMED FOR THIS.
NOW HOW'D-
NOW WHAT!?!

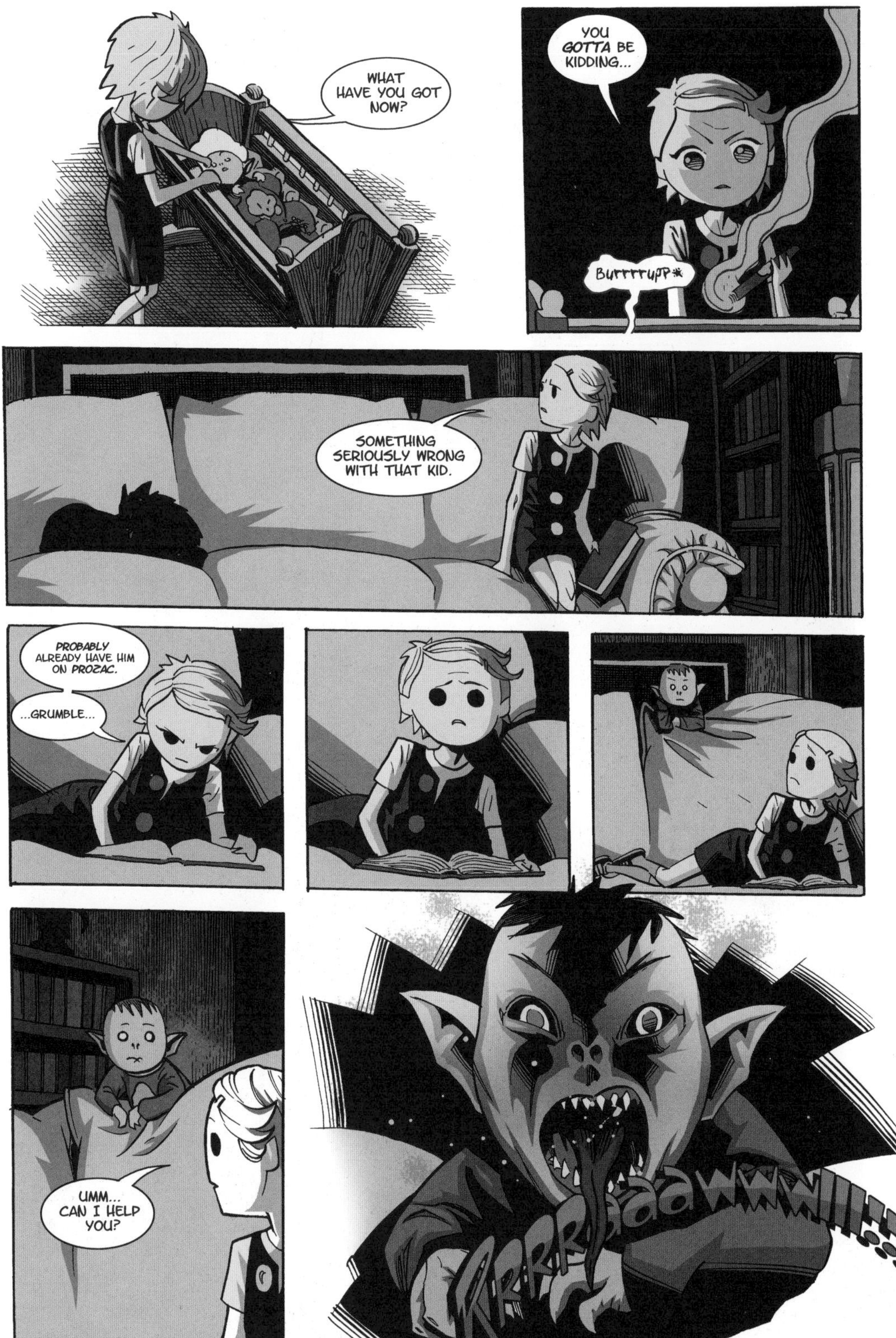
WHAT HAVE YOU GOT NOW?
YOU GOTTA BE KIDDING...
BurrrrupP
SOMETHING SERIOUSLY WRONG WITH THAT KID.
PROBABLY ALREADY HAVE HIM ON PROZAC.
...GRUMBLE...
UMM... CAN I HELP YOU?
RRRRaaawww!!!

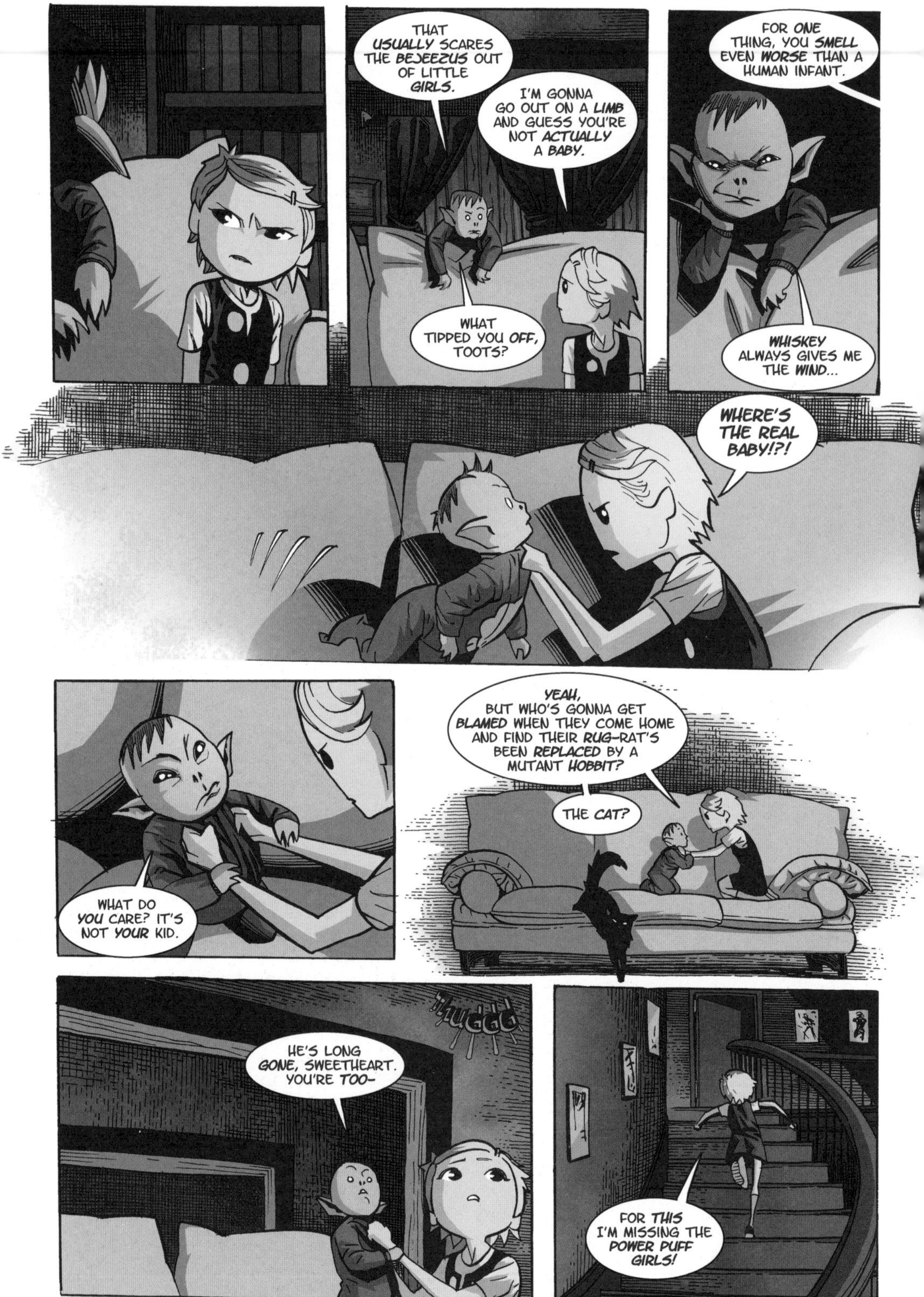
THAT USUALLY SCARES THE BEJEEZUS OUT OF LITTLE GIRLS.
I'M GONNA GO OUT ON A LIMB AND GUESS YOU'RE NOT ACTUALLY A BABY.
WHAT TIPPED YOU OFF, TOOTS?
FOR ONE THING, YOU SMELL EVEN WORSE THAN A HUMAN INFANT.
WHISKEY ALWAYS GIVES ME THE WIND...
WHERE'S THE REAL BABY!?!
WHAT DO YOU CARE? IT'S NOT YOUR KID.
YEAH, BUT WHO'S GONNA GET BLAMED WHEN THEY COME HOME AND FIND THEIR RUG-RAT'S BEEN REPLACED BY A MUTANT HOBBIT?
THE CAT?
THUGGG
HE'S LONG GONE, SWEETHEART. YOU'RE TOO-
FOR THIS I'M MISSING THE POWER PUFF GIRLS!

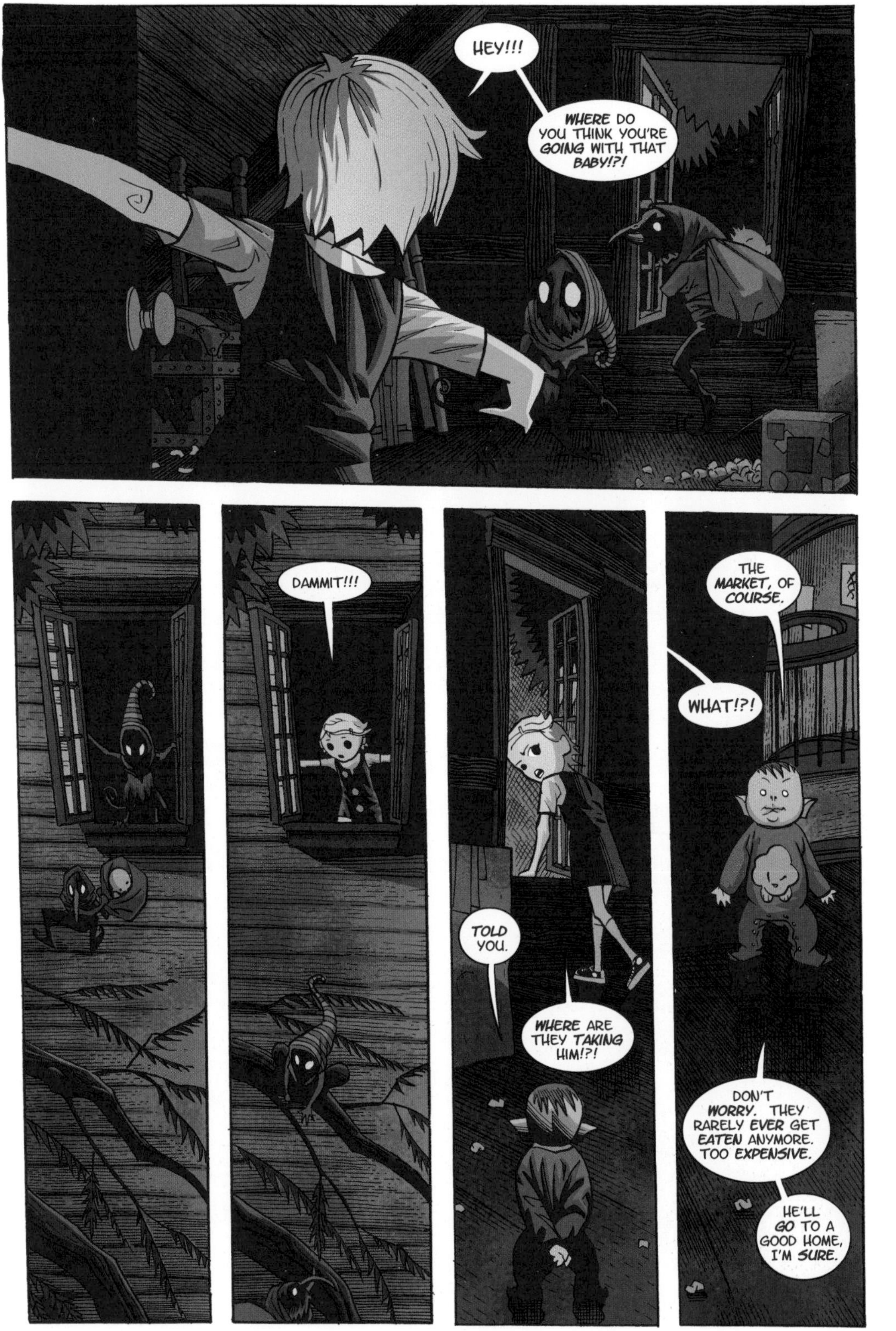
HEY!!!
WHERE DO YOU THINK YOU'RE GOING WITH THAT BABY!?!
DAMMIT!!!
TOLD YOU.
WHERE ARE THEY TAKING HIM!?!
WHAT!?!
THE MARKET, OF COURSE.
DON'T WORRY. THEY RARELY EVER GET EATEN ANYMORE. TOO EXPENSIVE.
HE'LL GO TO A GOOD HOME, I'M SURE.

OH, THIS IS JUST GONNA BE *WAY* TOO MUCH *FUN*...

WHOOPS...

I DO KNOW HOW TO PLAY *HIDE* AND *SEEK*, YA KNOW.

COMFY?

LET'S TALK ABOUT THAT BABY, SHALL WE?

≥BLEARGH≤

I CAN'T. I'M SWORN TO SECRECY.

YOU SURE?

TO *TALK* OF THESE THINGS WITH MORTALS IS FORBIDDEN.

YES

FINE.

YAAAAAAAAHHHH!!!

FEEL LIKE TALKING *NOW*?

IT'S IN THE CHANGELING UNION *BYLAWS*.

I'LL LOSE MY *PENSION*!

HAVE IT *YOUR* WAY.

GAÀAAAAAAHHHH!!!

OOOF, I'M GONNA BARF!

BE MY *GUEST*. WE'RE GONNA BE SPINNING ALL *NIGHT*.

ENOUGH!

WHO *SAID* THAT!?!

WHO'S *THERE*?

I'LL TELL YOU WHERE THEY TOOK THE CHILD, IF *THAT'S* WHAT IT TAKES TO GET SOME *PEACE* IN THIS HOUSE.

...HUH?

GONNA BE ONE OF THOSE *NIGHTS*, I GUESS.

SO, BOO, YOU WERE FILLING ME IN ON THIS *MUNCHKIN'S* LITTLE DEAL?

IT'S AN *ANCIENT PRACTICE*. A *CHANGELING* TAKES THE *PLACE* OF THE STOLEN CHILD.

USUALLY THE PARENTS ARE NEVER THE *WISER*.

GREAT. GIVE AWAY THE WHOLE *SHOW*, WHY DON'T YOU.

HAH!!!

OH, IT'S YOU.

HELLO, *BUTTERWORM*. WE WERE JUST TAKING A *STROLL* DOWN TO *GOBLIN* TOWN.

BUT IT'S *FORBIDDEN* FOR...

THAT'S WHAT WE TOLD HER.

OKAY. BEEN NICE KNOWIN' YE.

YE LITTLE BRAT.

GEE, THANKS.

SO WHAT DO THE *NIGHT THINGS* WANT WITH *YUPPIE-LARVAE* ANYWAY?

I COULDN'T BEGIN TO IMAGINE. I CERTAINLY HAVE NO USE FOR THEM.

THEY FETCH A GOOD *PRICE* ON THE DARK *MARKET*. THE ELDER ONES *RAISE* THEM AS THEIR *OWN*.

NICE. SO, BOO, WHAT'S YOUR STORY, ANYWAY?

NO *STORY*, MADAM. JUST A CAT.

JUST YOUR *GARDEN VARIETY* TALKING *HOUSE CAT*. *GOTCHA*.

CONSIDERING YOUR *LINEAGE*, MISS *CRUMRIN*, I'M *SURPRISED* HOW LITTLE YOU *KNOW* OF THE WORLD.

UH HUH.

HEY. WHY DIDN'T YOU *STOP* THOSE GUYS WHEN THEY WERE *KIDNAPPING* THE BABY?

IS IT MY *BUSINESS?*

YOU ARE THE FINCHES' *CAT* AREN'T YOU? WHAT ABOUT *LOYALTY?*

IF THEY'D WANTED *LOYALTY,* THEY'D HAVE GOTTEN A *DOG.* I STAY OUT OF *THEIR* AFFAIRS, AND *THEY* STAY OUT OF *MINE.*

THIS IS IT.

FOR A MOMENT, COURTNEY GAZED, TRANSFIXED, INTO THE VELVET DARKNESS OF THE TUNNEL. SHE SUSPECTED THAT SHE WAS ABOUT TO BITE OFF MORE THAN SHE COULD CHEW.

YET, SHE HAD LITTLE CHOICE BUT TO PRESS ON, IN THE HOPES THAT HER WITS AND HER LUCK WOULDN'T FAIL HER.

Goblin Town

REMEMBER, CHILD. TAKE *NO* FOOD *NOR* DRINK ONCE YOU PASS *WITHIN.*

YOU TREAD ON *DANGEROUS GROUND* HERE.

NOT SO FAST, SHORTY.

WELL, GOOD *LUCK,* KIDDO. I'LL JUST BE ON MY *WAY.*

YOU'RE GONNA TAKE ME *RIGHT* TO HIM.

BUT...

OR WE CAN SEE WHAT *HAPPENS* WHEN WE PUT THE BABY IN THE *MICROWAVE.*

...GRUMBLE...

THAT'S THE *SPIRIT.*

DESPITE HER BRAVADO, COURTNEY WAS FIGHTING OFF A BRIEF IMPULSE TO RUN SCREAMING INTO THE NIGHT.

TAKING A DEEP BREATH, SHE RESOLVED HERSELF TO THE TASK. "AFTER ALL," SHE THOUGHT TO HERSELF, "THIS CAN'T BE AS BAD AS CHANGING DIAPERS...".

WHO GOES THERE?

WE SMELL A *MORTAL* MAIDEN.

CHANGELING, ARE THE PATHS OF THE *NIGHT* FOR *MORTAL* FEET?

WHY DID YOU BRING THIS CHILD?

UH... NO, NO, SHE'S A... *WOOD NYMPH,* SEE?

IS SHE?

THAT'S RIGHT. I LOST MY WINGS IN A FREAK ACCIDENT, OKAY?

BACK OFF!

VERY CONVINCING.

SHUT UP!

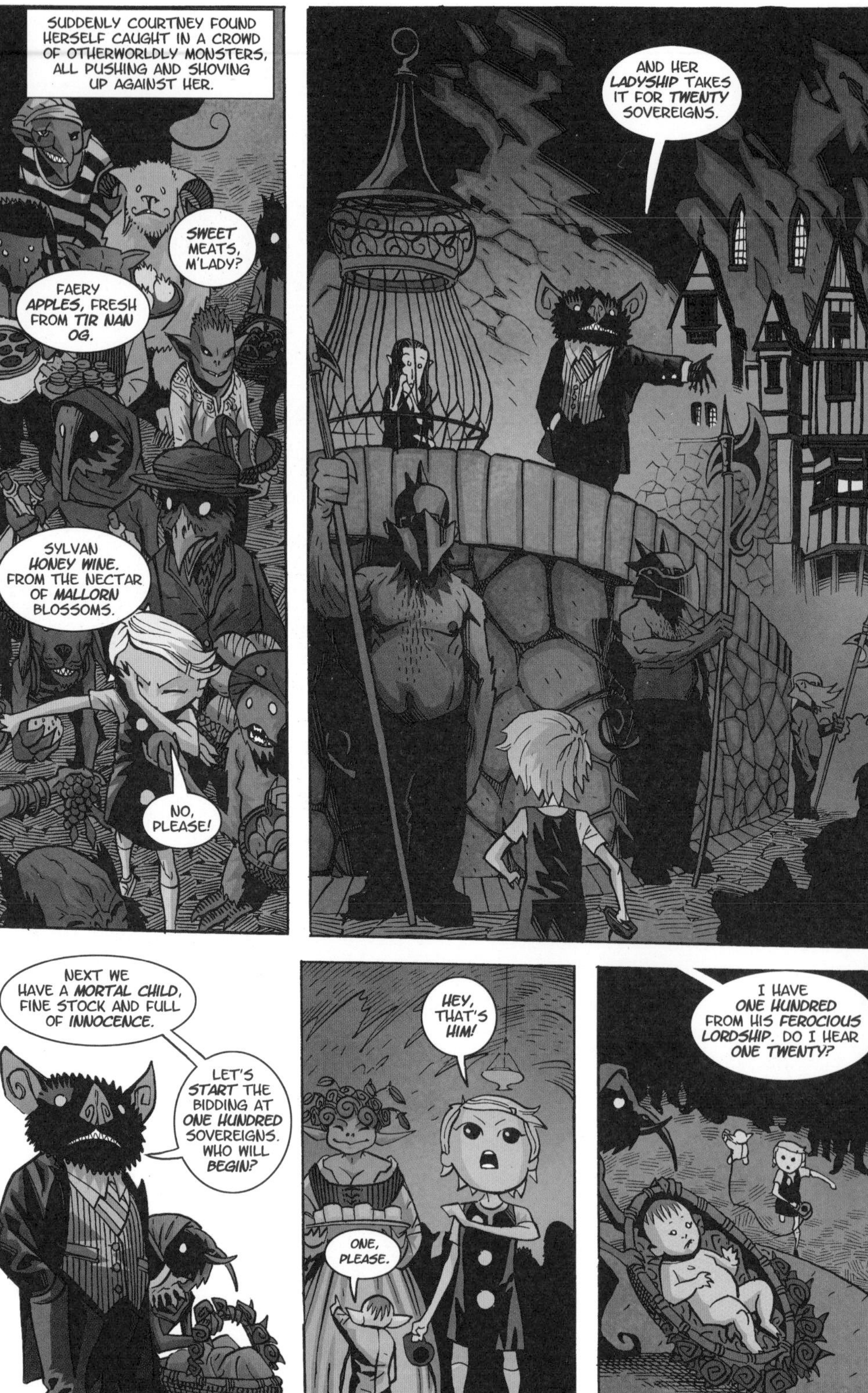
SUDDENLY COURTNEY FOUND HERSELF CAUGHT IN A CROWD OF OTHERWORLDLY MONSTERS, ALL PUSHING AND SHOVING UP AGAINST HER.
SWEET MEATS, M'LADY?
FAERY APPLES, FRESH FROM TIR NAN OG.
SYLVAN HONEY WINE. FROM THE NECTAR OF MALLORN BLOSSOMS.
NO, PLEASE!
AND HER LADYSHIP TAKES IT FOR TWENTY SOVEREIGNS.
NEXT WE HAVE A MORTAL CHILD, FINE STOCK AND FULL OF INNOCENCE.
LET'S START THE BIDDING AT ONE HUNDRED SOVEREIGNS. WHO WILL BEGIN?
HEY, THAT'S HIM!
ONE, PLEASE.
I HAVE ONE HUNDRED FROM HIS FEROCIOUS LORDSHIP. DO I HEAR ONE TWENTY?

WE HAVE AN EAGER BUYER, FOLKS!

I'M SORRY, YOUNG LADY, YOU'LL HAVE TO MAKE A BID.

THAT'S MY BABY!!!

I CAN'T BELIEVE I JUST SAID THAT.

INDEED IT IS, FOR A MERE ONE HUNDRED TWENTY SOVEREIGNS.

ALE?

FRESH BREAD?

EXOTIC SPICES?

NO!!!

≈COUGH≈ ≈COUGH≈ ≈COUGH≈...

≈CHOKE≈

HERE, DRINK THIS.

≈COUGH≈

THANKS.

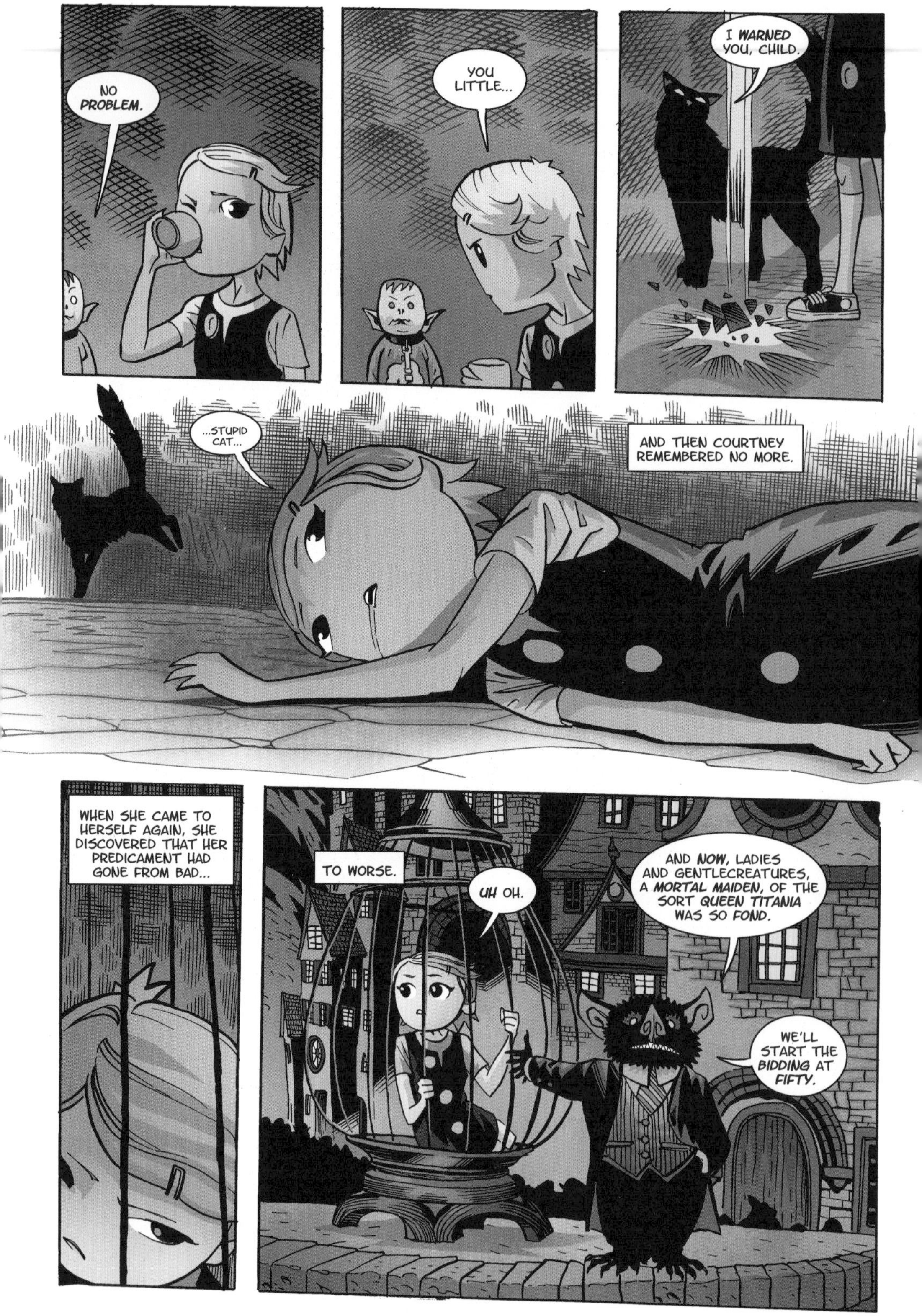
NO PROBLEM.
YOU LITTLE...
I WARNED YOU, CHILD.
...STUPID CAT...
AND THEN COURTNEY REMEMBERED NO MORE.
WHEN SHE CAME TO HERSELF AGAIN, SHE DISCOVERED THAT HER PREDICAMENT HAD GONE FROM BAD...
TO WORSE.
UH OH.
AND NOW, LADIES AND GENTLECREATURES, A MORTAL MAIDEN, OF THE SORT QUEEN TITANIA WAS SO FOND.
WE'LL START THE BIDDING AT FIFTY.

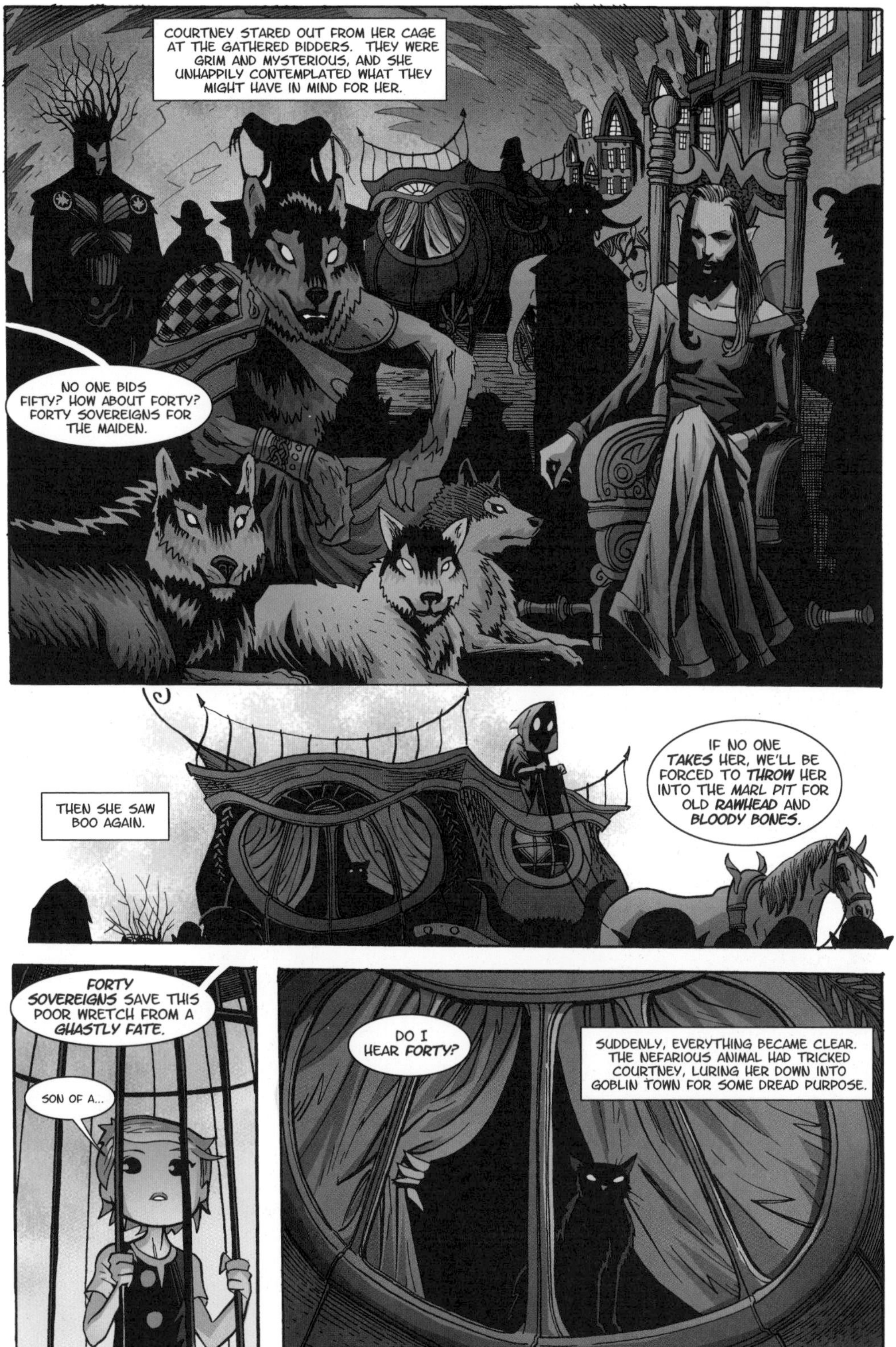
COURTNEY STARED OUT FROM HER CAGE AT THE GATHERED BIDDERS. THEY WERE GRIM AND MYSTERIOUS, AND SHE UNHAPPILY CONTEMPLATED WHAT THEY MIGHT HAVE IN MIND FOR HER.
NO ONE BIDS FIFTY? HOW ABOUT FORTY? FORTY SOVEREIGNS FOR THE MAIDEN.
THEN SHE SAW BOO AGAIN.
IF NO ONE TAKES HER, WE'LL BE FORCED TO THROW HER INTO THE MARL PIT FOR OLD RAWHEAD AND BLOODY BONES.
FORTY SOVEREIGNS SAVE THIS POOR WRETCH FROM A GHASTLY FATE.
SON OF A...
DO I HEAR FORTY?
SUDDENLY, EVERYTHING BECAME CLEAR. THE NEFARIOUS ANIMAL HAD TRICKED COURTNEY, LURING HER DOWN INTO GOBLIN TOWN FOR SOME DREAD PURPOSE.

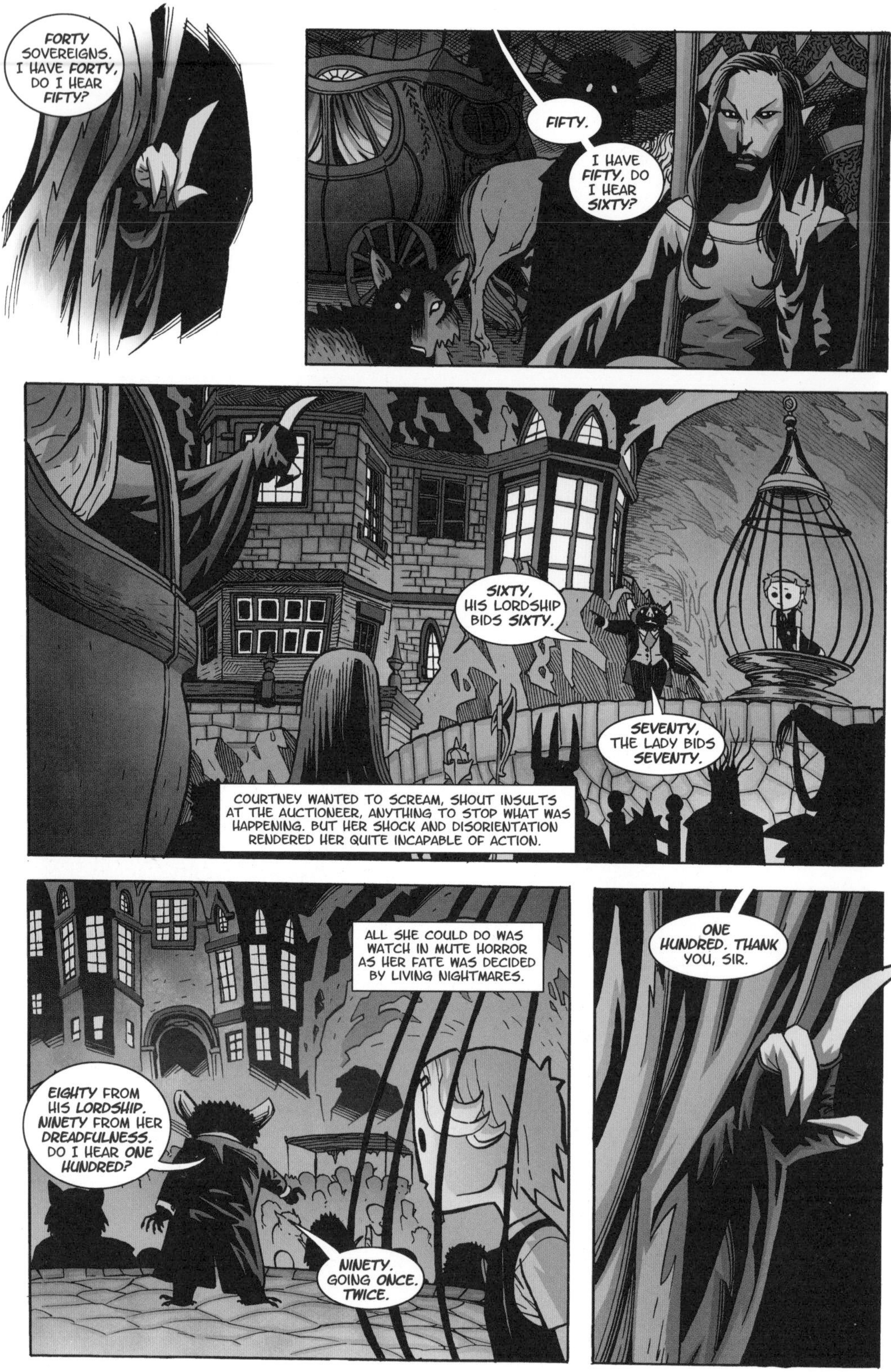

FORTY SOVEREIGNS. I HAVE FORTY, DO I HEAR FIFTY?
FIFTY.
I HAVE FIFTY, DO I HEAR SIXTY?
SIXTY, HIS LORDSHIP BIDS SIXTY.
SEVENTY, THE LADY BIDS SEVENTY.
COURTNEY WANTED TO SCREAM, SHOUT INSULTS AT THE AUCTIONEER, ANYTHING TO STOP WHAT WAS HAPPENING. BUT HER SHOCK AND DISORIENTATION RENDERED HER QUITE INCAPABLE OF ACTION.
ALL SHE COULD DO WAS WATCH IN MUTE HORROR AS HER FATE WAS DECIDED BY LIVING NIGHTMARES.
EIGHTY FROM HIS LORDSHIP. NINETY FROM HER DREADFULNESS. DO I HEAR ONE HUNDRED?
NINETY. GOING ONCE. TWICE.
ONE HUNDRED. THANK YOU, SIR.

YOU SET ME *UP*, DIDN'T YOU?

I DID *WARN* YOU, MADAM.

GOBLIN TOWN IS *NO* PLACE FOR MORTALS.

WHAT I *GET* FOR *TRUSTING* A TALKING CAT.

PERHAPS...

AS THEY PULLED AWAY AND DROVE OFF INTO THE DARK TUNNELS, THE FULL HORROR OF HER SITUATION SWEPT OVER COURTNEY.

IT'S *JUST*... NOT FAIR.

AFTER A TIME, THE CARRIAGE SLOWED TO A HALT, AND ITS SOLE OCCUPANT STEPPED OUT.

OH *CRAP*.

AS COURTNEY'S CAPTOR APPROACHED, HER TERROR BECAME WILD PANIC. SHE REALIZED NOW THAT NOTHING SHORT OF A MIRACLE COULD SAVE HER.

UNCLE A, WHERE ARE YOU?

I NEED SOME *HELP* HERE.

I'M RIGHT *HERE*, COURTNEY.

YOU'RE *NOT ESPECIALLY SHARP* TODAY, ARE YOU?

BUT... *HOW DID* YOU...?

YOUR LITTLE *FRIEND* HERE TIPPED ME OFF.

AND LUCKY FOR *YOU* THAT HE *DID*.

I WOULD NEVER HAVE *IMAGINED* A CLEVER GIRL LIKE *YOU* COULD *GET HERSELF* INTO SUCH AN *ABSURD* PREDICAMENT.

AND *WHAT WAS* I *SUPPOSED* TO DO?

EXPLAIN TO *MRS. FINCH* THAT HER BABY'S BEEN *KIDNAPPED* AND REPLACED BY AN *EVIL MUPPET*?

EVELYN FINCH? SHE'D *NEVER* NOTICE.

BUT THE *BABY!* HE'S BEEN *SOLD* TO THAT FREAKY *LIZARD LADY.*

I'M *TOUCHED* BY YOUR *CONCERN*, BUT THESE THINGS *HAPPEN*, COURTNEY.

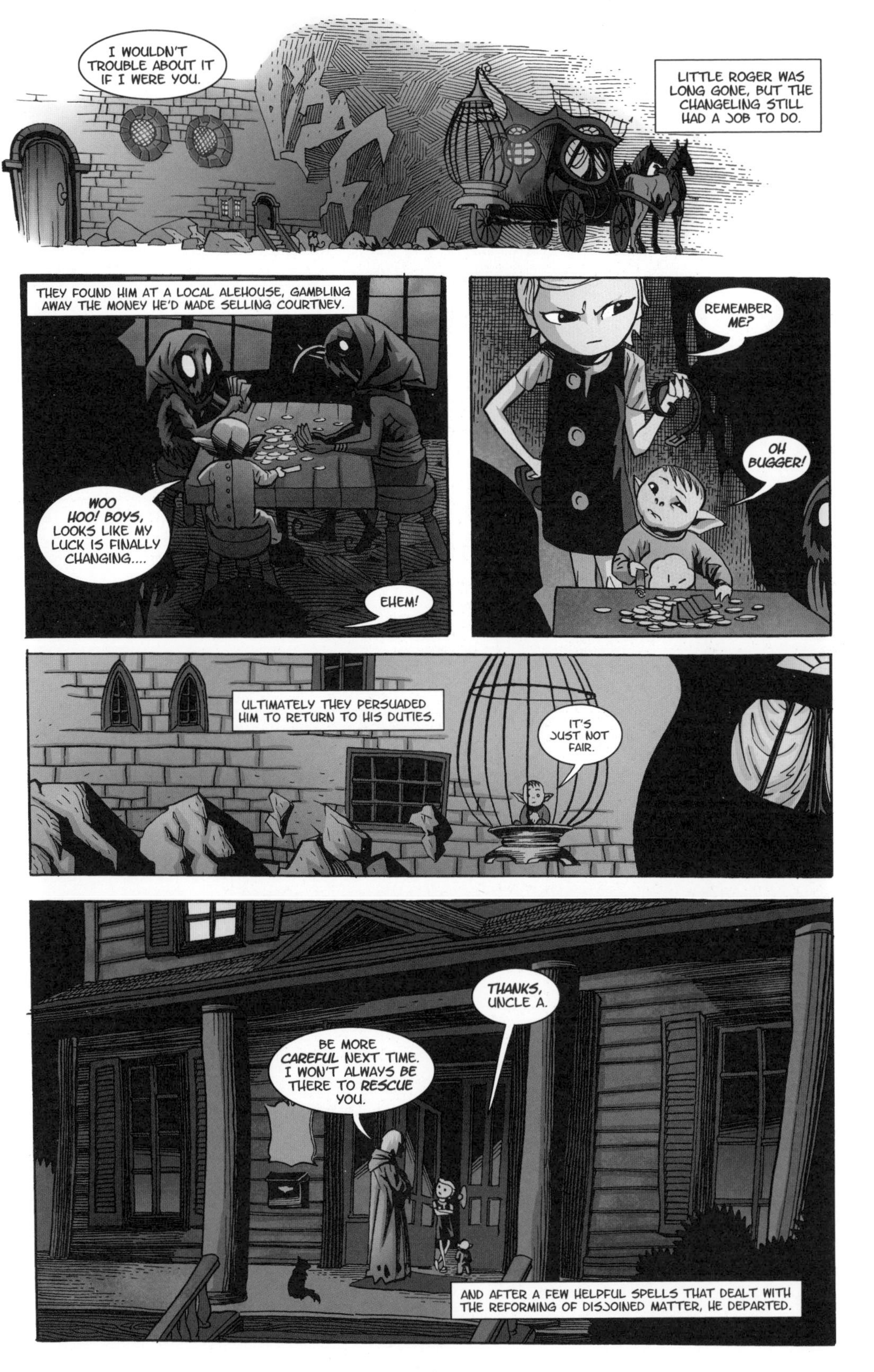
I WOULDN'T TROUBLE ABOUT IT IF I WERE YOU.
LITTLE ROGER WAS LONG GONE, BUT THE CHANGELING STILL HAD A JOB TO DO.
THEY FOUND HIM AT A LOCAL ALEHOUSE, GAMBLING AWAY THE MONEY HE'D MADE SELLING COURTNEY.
WOO HOO! BOYS, LOOKS LIKE MY LUCK IS FINALLY CHANGING....
EHEM!
REMEMBER ME?
OH BUGGER!
ULTIMATELY THEY PERSUADED HIM TO RETURN TO HIS DUTIES.
IT'S JUST NOT FAIR.
THANKS, UNCLE A.
BE MORE CAREFUL NEXT TIME. I WON'T ALWAYS BE THERE TO RESCUE YOU.
AND AFTER A FEW HELPFUL SPELLS THAT DEALT WITH THE REFORMING OF DISJOINED MATTER, HE DEPARTED.

OH, HEY. DID YOU CRAZY KIDS HAVE **FUN** TONIGHT?

WE SURE DID. SO COULD YOU COME BACK AGAIN NEXT WEEK?

FIFTY DOLLARS A **NIGHT**...

NO PROBLEM.

Chapter Four

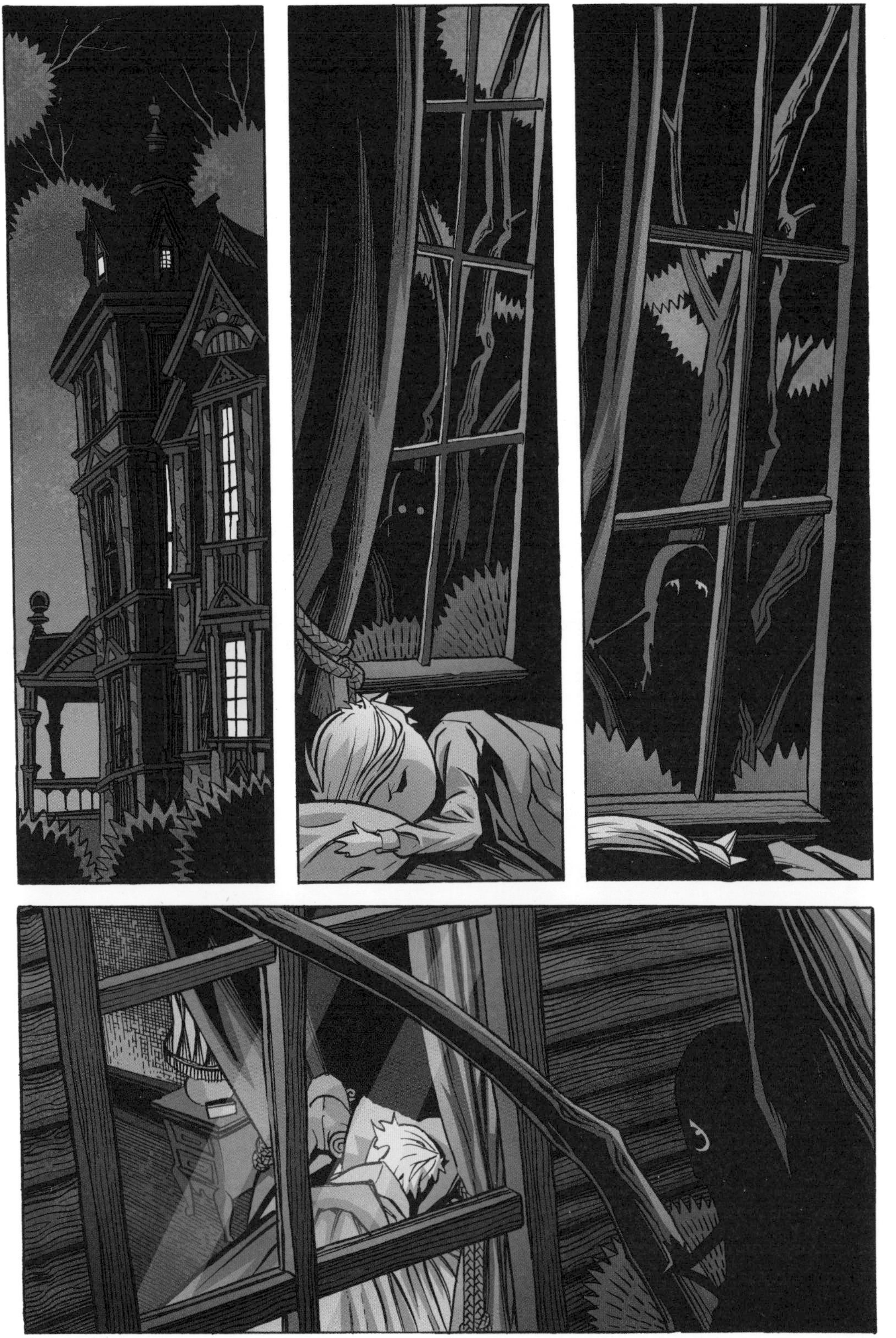

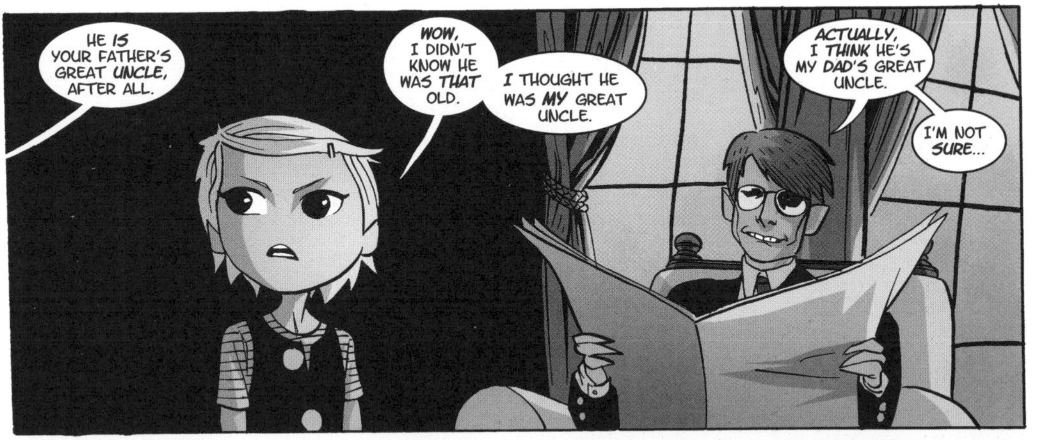
HE IS YOUR FATHER'S GREAT UNCLE, AFTER ALL.
WOW, I DIDN'T KNOW HE WAS THAT OLD.
I THOUGHT HE WAS MY GREAT UNCLE.
ACTUALLY, I THINK HE'S MY DAD'S GREAT UNCLE.
I'M NOT SURE...

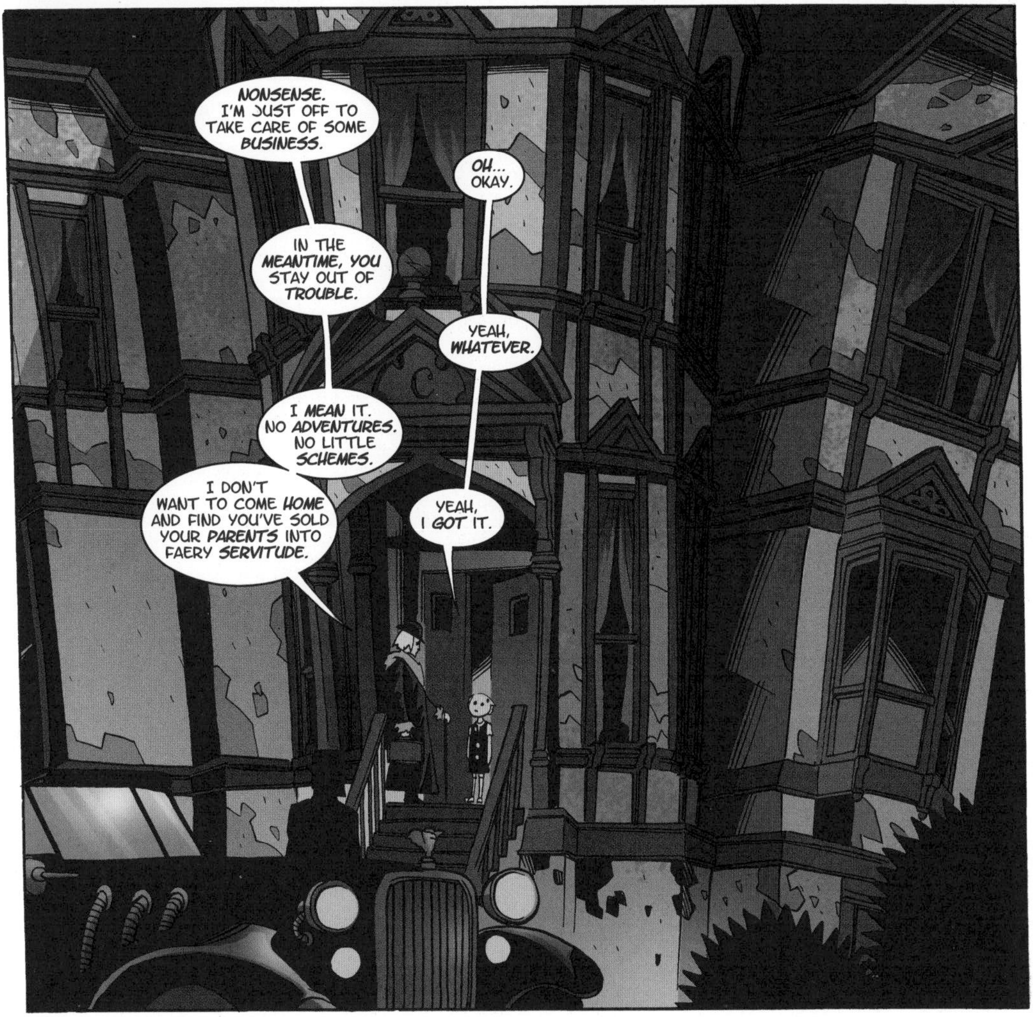
NONSENSE. I'M JUST OFF TO TAKE CARE OF SOME BUSINESS.
OH... OKAY.
IN THE MEANTIME, YOU STAY OUT OF TROUBLE.
YEAH, WHATEVER.
I MEAN IT. NO ADVENTURES. NO LITTLE SCHEMES.
I DON'T WANT TO COME HOME AND FIND YOU'VE SOLD YOUR PARENTS INTO FAERY SERVITUDE.
YEAH, I GOT IT.

ARE YOU *LISTENING TO ME,* COURTNEY?

MMMM...

I'LL BE BACK *SOON. TWO WEEKS* AT THE OUTSIDE.

NO BIGGY, UNCLE A. I GOT *MOM* AND DAD TO KEEP ME ENTERTAINED.

AND SO THE DAYS WENT BY. BUT COURTNEY FOUND HERSELF MISSING THE STRANGE OLD MAN MUCH MORE THAN SHE EXPECTED.

SHE TRIED TO FALL BACK ON HER OLD HABITS.

SPOKEN TO MRS. *FINCH* LATELY?

SAW HER AT THE *GROCERY STORE,* BUT I COULDN'T CATCH UP.

FOR A WOMAN PUSHING A *SHOPPING* CART FILLED WITH *WINE,* SHE SURE CAN MOVE *FAST.*

KNOW WHAT YOU MEAN. JEB'S THE SAME WAY.

I JUST CAN'T KEEP UP WITH HIM JOGGING. THEY REALLY *PUSH* THEMSELVES.

IT'S SO INSPIRING. SUCH GREAT PEOPLE.

BUT WATCHING HER PARENTS DIDN'T PROVIDE AS MUCH DIVERSION AS IT ONCE HAD.

NOT HAVING REAL FRIENDS WAS SOMETHING THAT COURTNEY HAD LEARNED TO LIVE WITH. BUT IT HAD ITS SHORTCOMINGS.

SO NOW IT'S *YOUR* TURN. TAKE THE DICE.

MUH!

TAKE 'EM.

MUH!

...GRUMBLE...

≈CRUNCH≈
≈CRUNCH≈
≈CRUNCH≈

FORGET IT.

YOU TOO, HANDSOME. OUT!

SLAMMM

AND SHE BEGAN TO WONDER WHY SHE HAD SO MUCH TROUBLE FINDING ANYBODY WORTH SPENDING TIME WITH.

Hillsborough Wine Merchant

Drive in Video

COURTNEY'S DESPONDENCY SLOWLY GREW. ALL AROUND HER, THE OTHER CHILDREN HAPPILY BABBLED AWAY...

comedy

CHECK IT OUT. THE LATEST.

DUDE!

AWESOME.

I WANT ONE.

Tight-wad 'fitness — open 24hrs

...AND ADULTS OCCUPIED THEMSELVES WITH INEXPLICABLE ACTIVITIES.

AND ONE...

TWO...

THREE...

FOUR...

COURTNEY WAS A PRACTICAL GIRL, AND IT BEGAN TO OCCUR TO HER THAT PERHAPS SHE WAS MISSING SOMETHING ABOUT THE WORLD. SOMETHING IMPORTANT.

AND BREATHE...

TWO...

THREE...

FOUR...

AFTER ALL, WHAT WAS MORE LIKELY? THAT THE WORLD WAS FILLED WITH COMPLETE DOOFUSES?

OR THAT THERE MIGHT BE SOMETHING WRONG WITH HER?

ONE MORNING, COURTNEY AWOKE AND FELT AS THOUGH HER DESPONDENCY HAD BECOME A PHYSICAL AILMENT.

BREAKFAST, COURTNEY!

MMMMPH.

DON'T *FEEL* GOOD.

SORRY, NOT BUYING *THAT* ONE. SEE YOU DOWNSTAIRS IN TEN MINUTES.

COURTNEY WRESTLED FOR THE STRENGTH TO RISE, BUT IT WAS NO USE. THANKFULLY, HER MOTHER SEEMED TO HAVE FORGOTTEN ABOUT HER.

BY EVENING, SHE SUMMONED ENOUGH STRENGTH TO GO DOWNSTAIRS. DINNER HAD BEEN EATEN, BUT SHE FOUND SOME LEFTOVERS IN THE KITCHEN.

STILL HUNGRY?

YOU LOOK *AWFUL*. MAYBE YOU ARE GETTING SICK.

I TRIED TO TELL YOU THIS *MORNING*.

YOU SHOULD *PROBABLY* STAY *HOME* TOMORROW.

THE NEXT MORNING SHE FELT EVEN WORSE. THIS TIME HER MOTHER DIDN'T BOTHER HER, AND ONCE AGAIN SHE SLEPT UNTIL EVENING.

SHE HAD NO APPETITE, BUT WORRIED ABOUT LOSING WHAT LITTLE STRENGTH SHE HAD LEFT.

SHE FORCED HERSELF TO TAKE THE LONG TREK DOWNSTAIRS.

HER FATHER WAS STILL AT THE DINNER TABLE, AS USUAL, READING THE WALL STREET JOURNAL AND PRETENDING TO UNDERSTAND IT.

HEY, HONEY.

YOU DON'T *LOOK* SO HOT. YOUR MOTHER *SAID* YOU WERE A LITTLE UNDER THE *WEATHER* LAST NIGHT.

YOU'RE *DEFINITELY* STAYING HOME TOMORROW.

THE UNSPOKEN THREAT OF A VISIT TO THE DOCTOR LOOMED MENACINGLY.

NO, *NO*, I'M OKAY.

SWEETIE, YOU'RE *NEVER* GOING TO GET *BETTER* IF YOU DON'T GET SOME *REST*.

THAT'S ABOUT *ALL* I'VE BEEN DOING.

WELL, CATHY KELLER'S MOM SAID YOU WERE OUT *SHOPPING* WITH THE *GIRLS* AFTER *SCHOOL* TODAY.

REALLY? DOES THAT *SOUND* LIKE ME?

GOOD POINT.

COME TO THINK OF IT, YOU REALLY HAVEN'T BEEN YOURSELF LATELY.

IT'S BEEN RATHER REFRESHING.

GEE, THANKS. CAN I EAT NOW?

DON'T OVERDO IT, DEAR. ISN'T THAT YOUR THIRD HELPING?

I KNEW ALL THAT PERFUME WOULD EVENTUALLY EAT AWAY HER BRAIN.

THE FOLLOWING MORNING, COURTNEY'S CONDITION STILL HADN'T IMPROVED. IF ANYTHING, SHE FELT WORSE THAN EVER. BUT FEAR OF DR. GRACE'S GHOULISH BEDSIDE MANNER SPURRED HER OUT OF BED.

I HAVE THE GRADES FOR YESTERDAY'S QUIZ. DON'T START CALLING *HARVARD* JUST YET, FOLKS.

Essay:
Describe your
last trip abroad

MRS. FINCH, WILL I BE ABLE TO TAKE A *MAKEUP* TEST?

DON'T BE SILLY, YOU DID GREAT.

WAY TO *GO*, COURTNEY.

GOOD *JOB*, MISS CRUMRIN. SEE WHAT YOU CAN DO WHEN YOU JUST *APPLY* YOURSELF?

YEAH. HEY, *THANKS* FOR HELPING ME OUT.

COURTNEY, NEEDLESS TO SAY, WAS TOO PERPLEXED TO ANSWER.

112

I REALLY DON'T THINK I'M *UP* FOR *RACKET-BALL* TODAY.

DOESN'T *SURPRISE* ME. YOU'VE REALLY BEEN *GOING* FOR IT THESE LAST COUPLE OF DAYS.

I HAVE?

DON'T BE SO *MODEST*. *OH*, BY THE *WAY*, YOUR *UNIFORM* IS HERE.

UNIFORM?

SURE. I HAD TO PULL A FEW *STRINGS* TO GET YOU ON THE TEAM THIS LATE, BUT YOUR *ENTHUSIASM* IMPRESSED ME.

I DON'T THINK ANYONE'S EVER *SAID* THAT TO ME BEFORE.

OF COURSE, IT WAS EASY TO WRITE OFF HER PARENTS' WEIRD BEHAVIOR AS BRAIN DAMAGE, BUT THIS WAS ANOTHER MATTER. HAD SHE GONE TO SCHOOL THE PREVIOUS DAY AND BEEN TOO SICK TO REMEMBER? IT DIDN'T MAKE SENSE.

YO! CRUMRIN!

HEY, COURTNEY.

HEY, GIRLFRIEND!

YOU COMING SHOPPING AGAIN TODAY?

MMMPH.

...GRUMBLE...

DESPITE HER GROWING CONFUSION, COURTNEY'S ENERGY SLOWLY DIMINISHED. BY LUNCHTIME, SHE COULD BARELY EAT.

AT LAST, EXHAUSTION OVERTOOK HER.

ZZZZZZZZZZZZZZZ...

SHE AWOKE HALF AN HOUR LATER, AND REALIZED SHE WAS LATE FOR CLASS.

BA!!

WA!?!

JUST NOT MY WEEK.

IT WAS ALL SHE COULD DO TO STRUGGLE BACK TO THE SCHOOLHOUSE.

BUT WHAT SHE SAW THERE STOPPED HER COLD.

CAN SOMEONE *TELL* ME *WHAT* ABOUT THIS SENTENCE IS INCORRECT?

COURTNEY?

IT'S "MY *AUNT,* WITH *WHOM* I TRAVELED TO PARIS", NOT "*WHO* I TRAVELED TO PARIS *WITH*".

VERY GOOD. YOU'RE REALLY ON THE BALL TODAY, YOUNG LADY.

THANK YOU, MRS. FINCH.

COURTNEY HAD NEVER BEEN SO HORRIFIED AS SHE WAS THAT MOMENT. AND A SECOND LATER...

...HER HORROR DOUBLED.

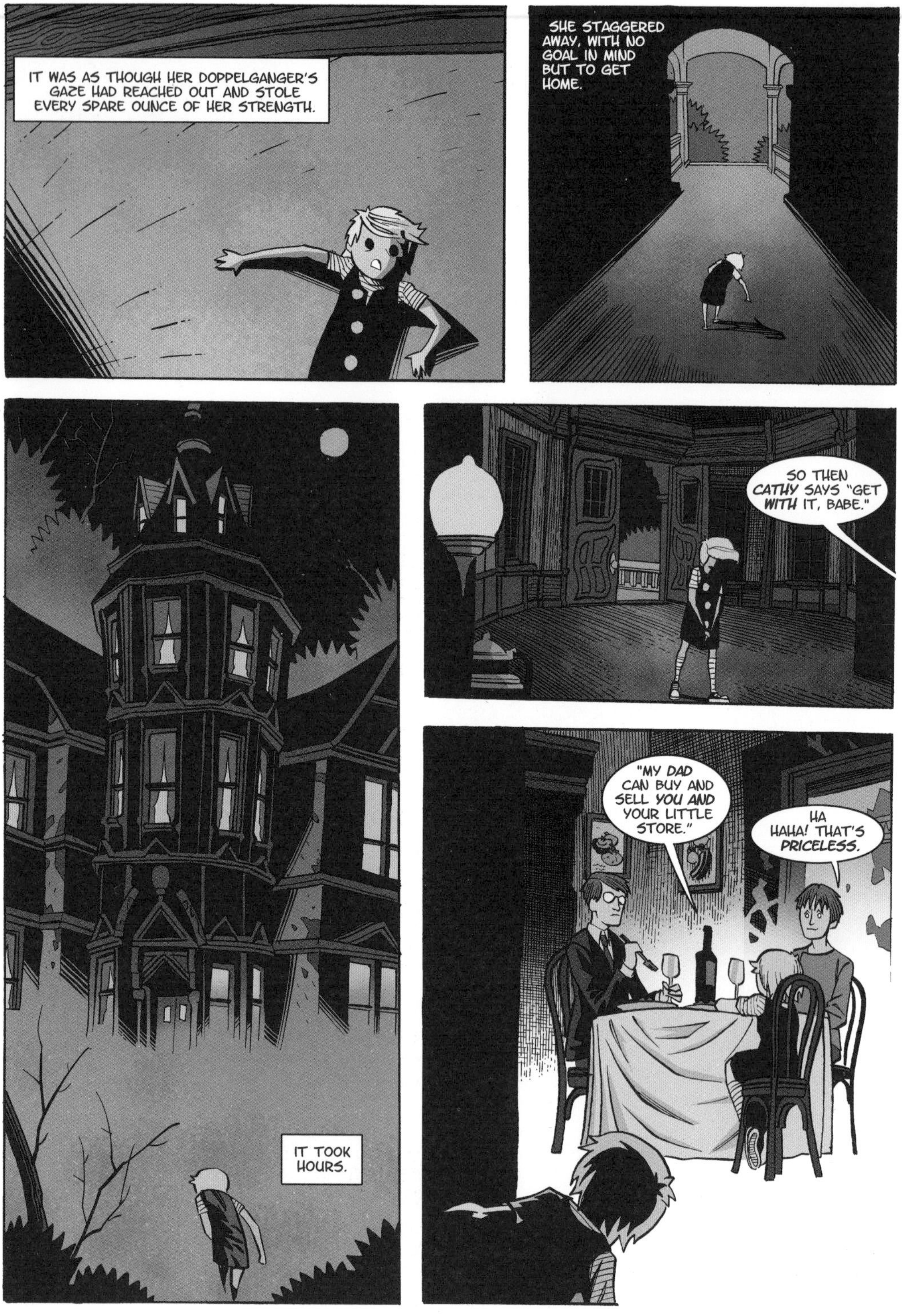

IT WAS AS THOUGH HER DOPPELGANGER'S GAZE HAD REACHED OUT AND STOLE EVERY SPARE OUNCE OF HER STRENGTH.
SHE STAGGERED AWAY, WITH NO GOAL IN MIND BUT TO GET HOME.
IT TOOK HOURS.
SO THEN CATHY SAYS "GET WITH IT, BABE."
"MY DAD CAN BUY AND SELL YOU AND YOUR LITTLE STORE."
HA HAHA! THAT'S PRICELESS.

TERROR AND REVULSION MIXED PAINFULLY IN COURTNEY'S GUT.

WITNESSING THE EXCHANGE BETWEEN THE IMPOSTER AND HER FAMILY, SHE SUDDENLY SAW JUST HOW OUT OF PLACE SHE HAD ALWAYS BEEN.

IT HAD USURPED HER LIFE EFFORTLESSLY AND WAS WELCOMED BY EVERYONE WITHOUT QUESTION.

AND WHY NOT?

WHAT REASON HAD THEY TO LIKE HER MORE THAN IT? WHAT DID SHE OFFER THE WORLD?

FOR ALL HER TRUE SELF MATTERED TO ANYONE...

...SHE MIGHT NEVER HAVE EXISTED AT ALL.

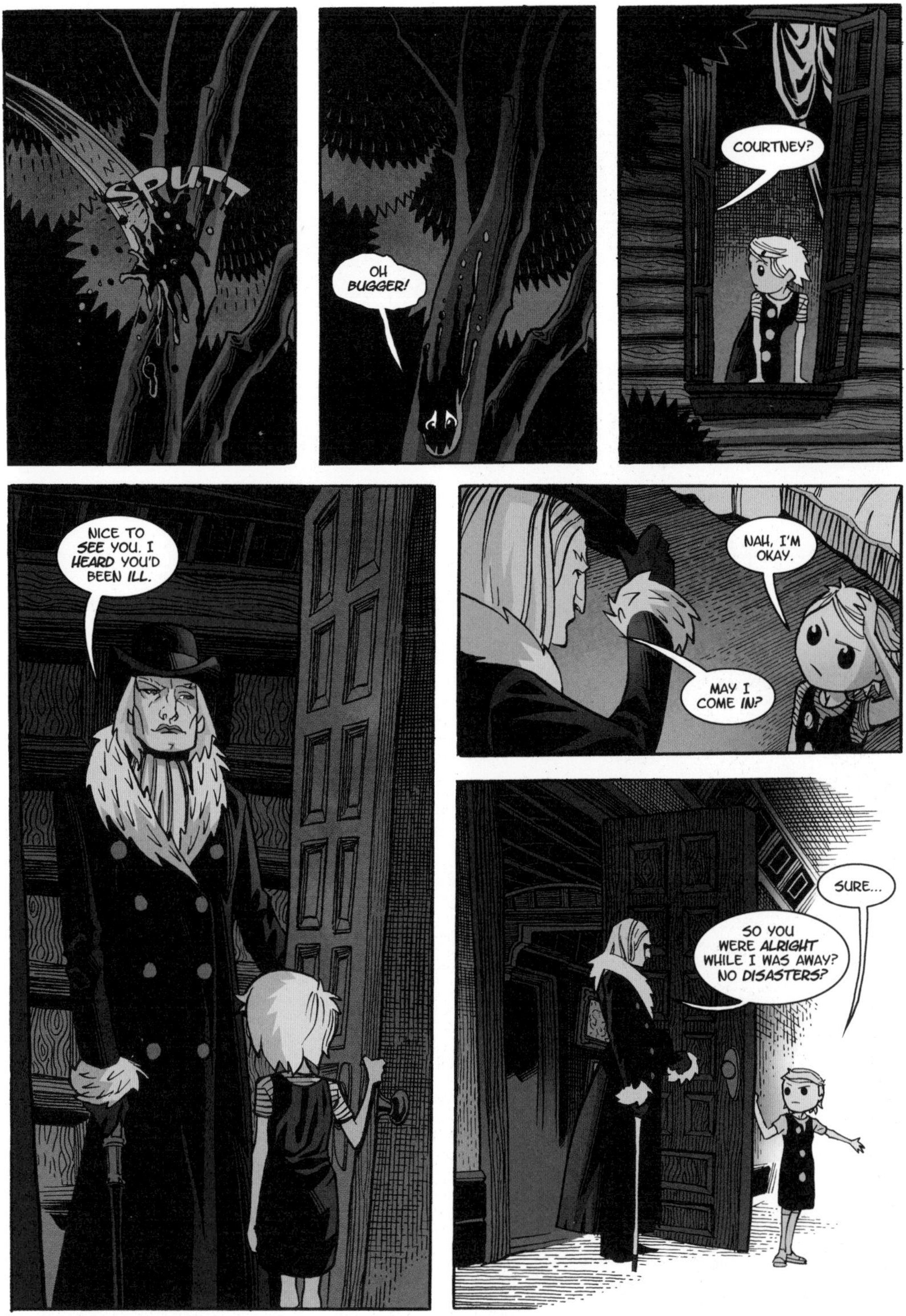
SPUTT
OH BUGGER!
COURTNEY?
NICE TO SEE YOU. I HEARD YOU'D BEEN ILL.
NAH, I'M OKAY.
MAY I COME IN?
SURE...
SO YOU WERE ALRIGHT WHILE I WAS AWAY? NO DISASTERS?

WELL, THAT'S THE STORY A' HOW YOUNG COURTNEY COME TO LIVE IN CRUMRIN HOUSE.

SHE AND OL' MAN CRUMRIN ARE THICK AS THIEVES NOW. NEVER THOUGHT A LITTLE BRAT LIKE 'ER COULD MELT 'IS ICY HEART.

THOUGH 'E TRIES TO KEEP 'ER AWAY FROM CERTAIN BOOKS.

YEH STILL HANGIN' ABOUT?

'ER FOLKS'RE STILL TRYIN' TE BE ALL POSH, FIT IN WITH THE NEIGHBORHOOD GENTRY.

BLEAGH!

MARK YEH, THEY THINK "BOURGEOIS" IS A BEDROOM.

BUT EVERYONE'S TUCKED IN THERE ALL COZY NOW, BLESS 'EM.

A'COURSE, IT WON'T LAST. NOT IN THIS NEIGHBORHOOD. THERE'RE BAD THINGS LURKIN' ABOUT.

WORSE EVEN THEN ME.

SO IF YEH COME BACK THIS WAY, WATCH YER STEP.

YEH AIN'T SEEN NOTHING YET.

Courtney Crumrin

By Ted Naifeh

The Night Things

Bonus Material & Cover Gallery

ALOYSIUS

COURTNEY

BOO

Initial character sketches for *Courtney Crumrin and the Night Things.*

NIGHT THINGS

THE WUG

Gritch

MUH

Courtney CRUMRIN

WENDEL

MR NOG

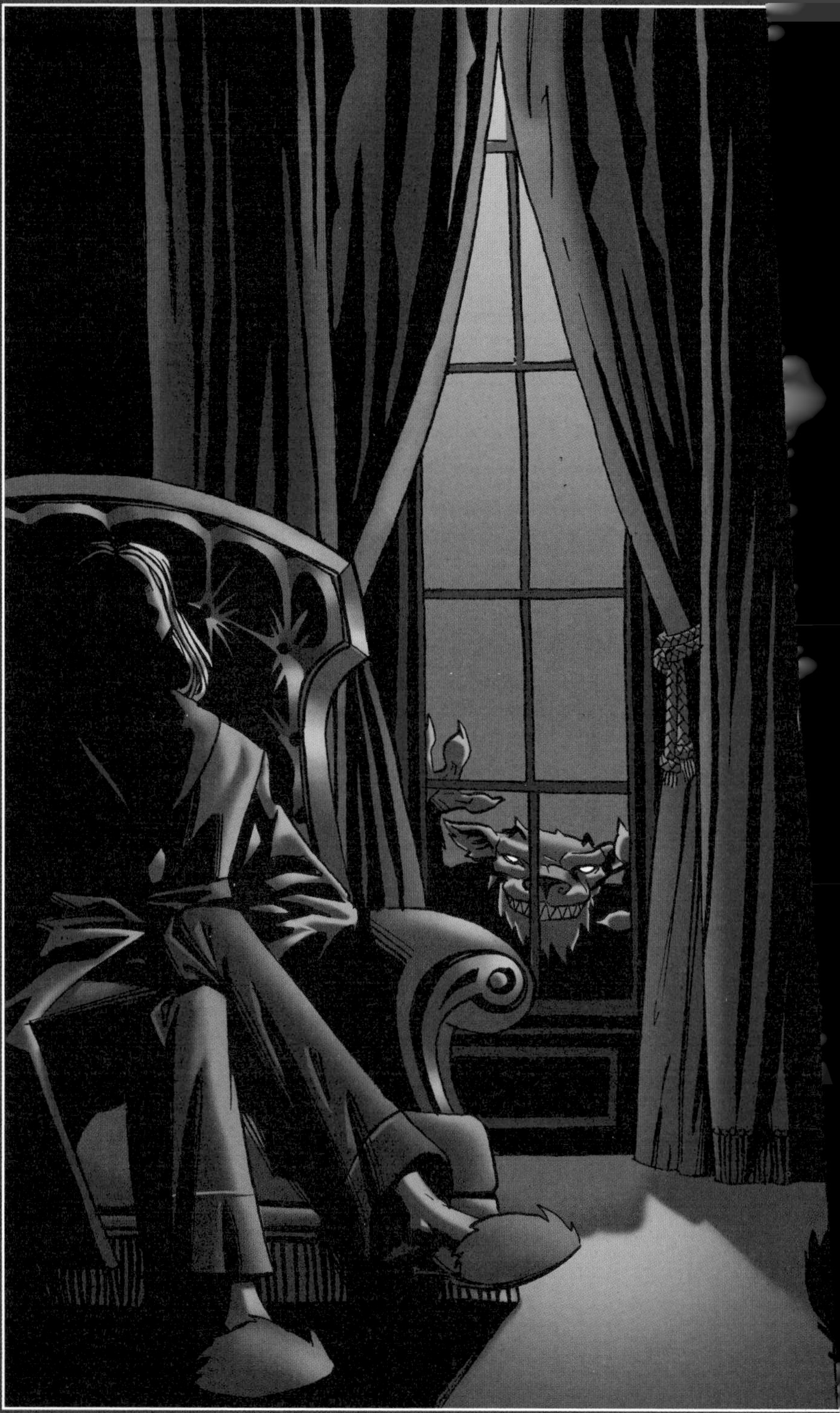

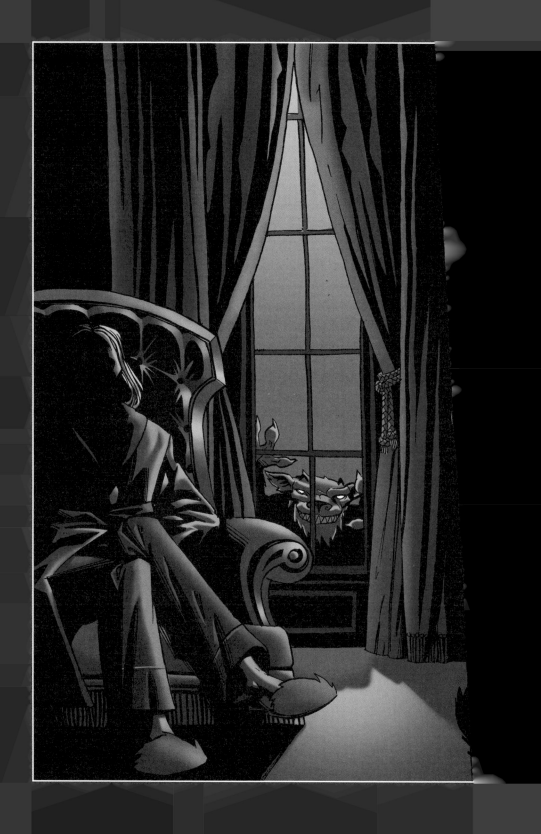

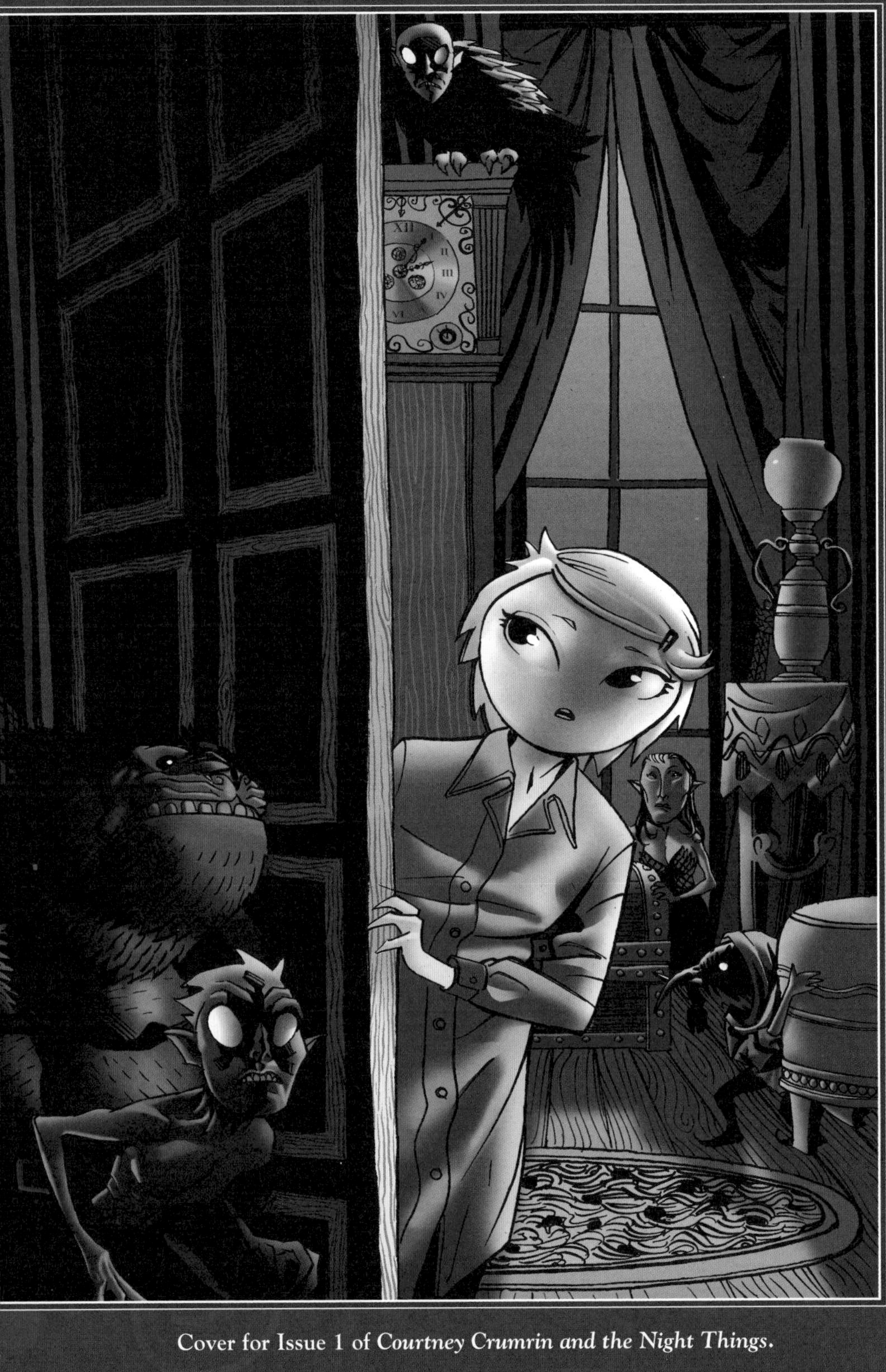

Cover for Issue 1 of *Courtney Crumrin and the Night Things.*

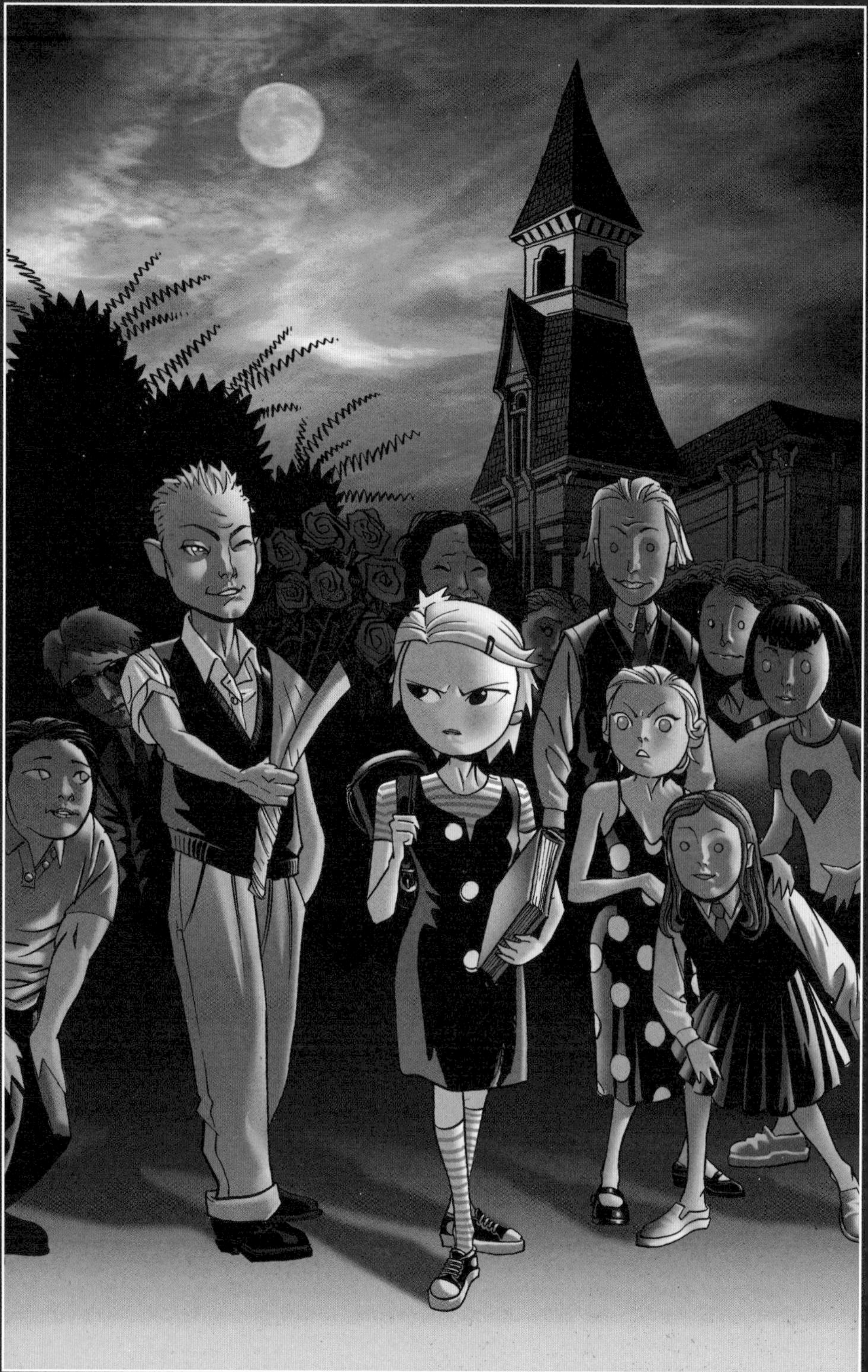

Cover for Issue 3 of Courtney Crumrin and the Night Things

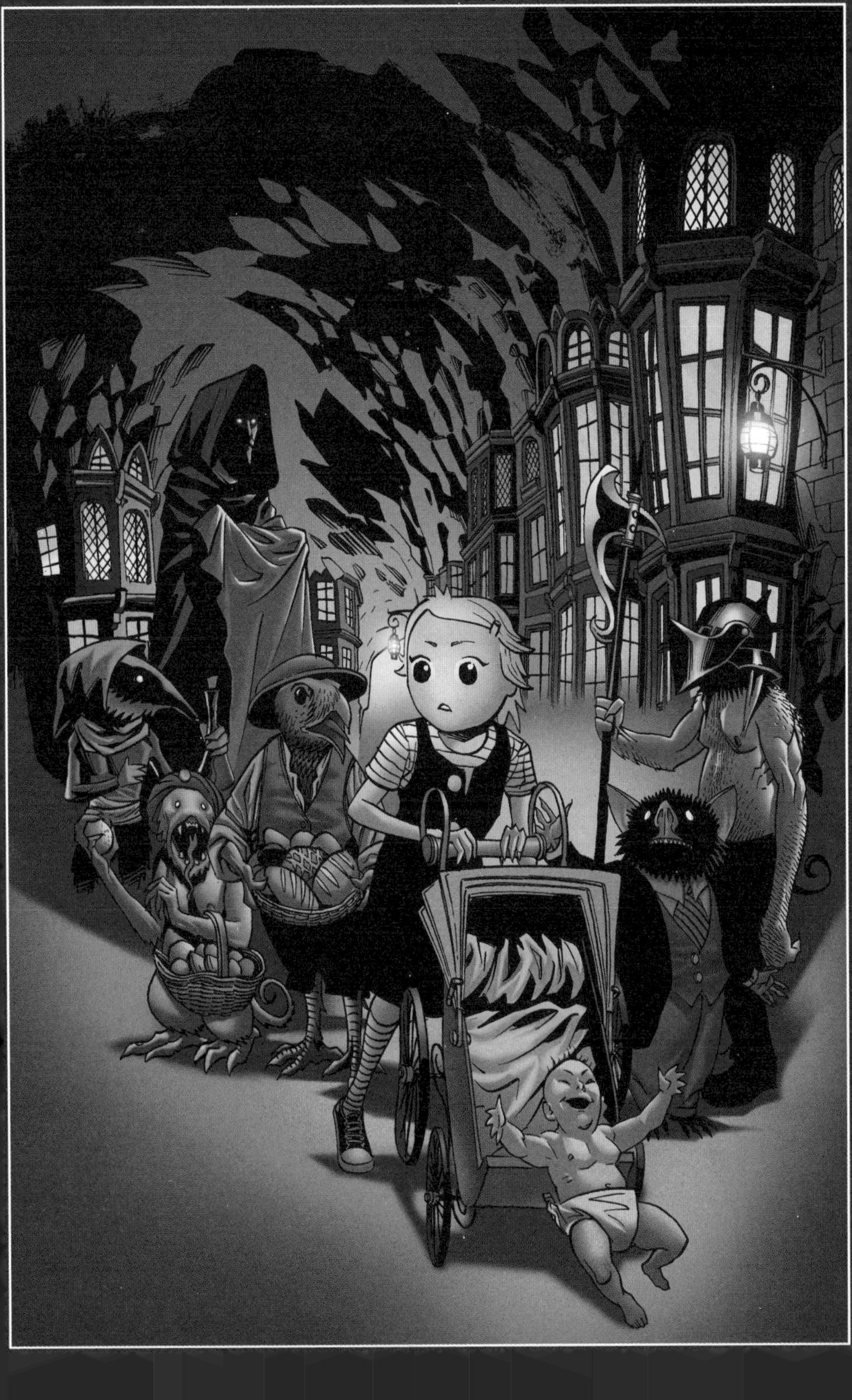

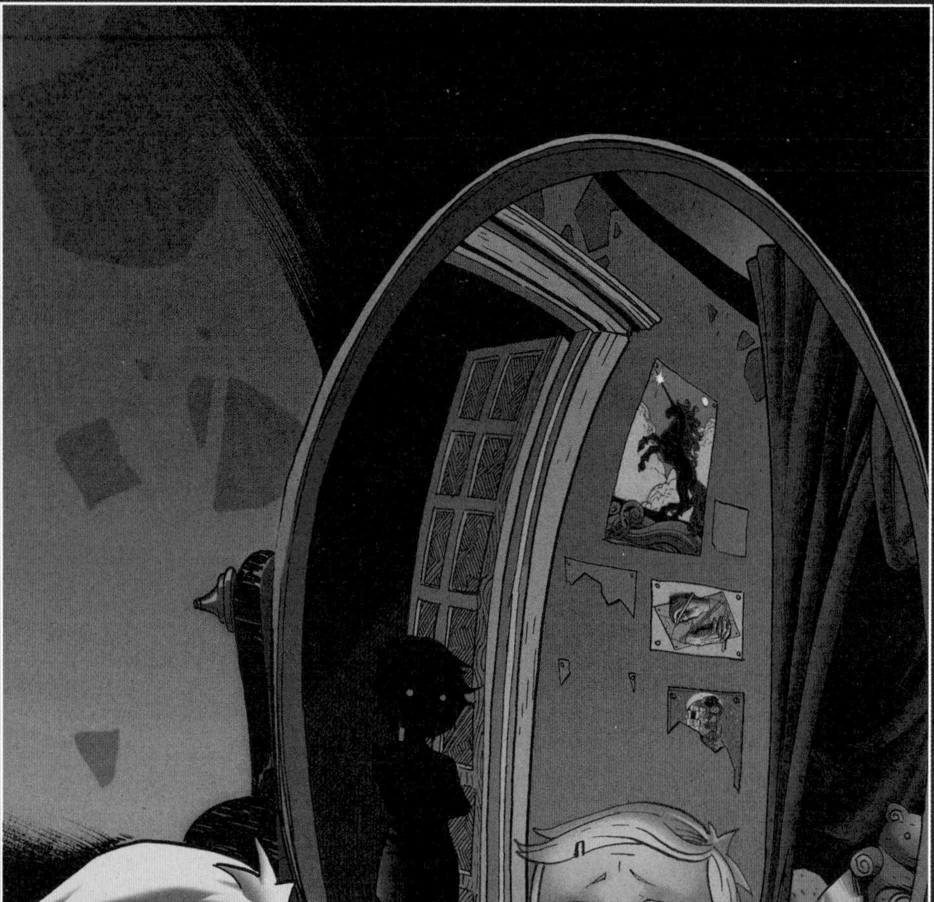

Cover for Issue [redacted]

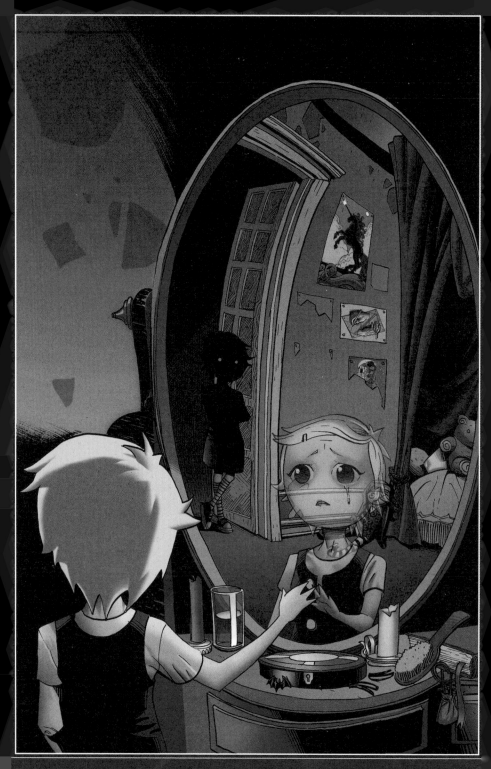